UNCOVERED!

Daily Devotionals from John's Gospel

James G. McCluskey

Unless otherwise indicated, Scripture quotations are from the World English Bible, a Public Domain Modern English translation of the Holy Bible. The World English Bible is based on the American Standard Version of the Holy Bible, first published in 1901.

ACKNOWLEDGMENTS

Few real accomplishments are ever achieved without the assistance and encouragement of others.

Thanks to Ann Lovell for her help in editing the first book of DAILY DEVOTIONALS from the Gospel of Mark, "UNWRAPPED". She suggested the title for that book. Ann is a published author. She has been an encourager to me in this process. When I ask her for some advice, she volunteered to edit the book for me.

Thanks to my son, Dr. Jay McCluskey, for accumulating the DAILY DEVOTIONALS and helping put them in the proper format. His positive words have been important in seeing this adventure through to the end. Now I am encouraging him to publish a book! Jay is Pastor of North Cleveland Baptist Church in Cleveland, Tennessee.

Thanks to all the first readers of these devotionals, my Facebook friends. The majority of them are members of Wallace Memorial Baptist Church. Their comments have kept me going. Both their daily feedback by commenting to the Facebook posts and their personal words have blessed me.

FOREWARD

I first wrote a Daily Devotional series for Lent, 2022, based on the Gospel of Mark. I first did these as a daily post on my Facebook page. At the end of the Lenten season several of my regular readers ask me if I would continue to do a Daily Devotional. These devotionals from the Gospel of John are the result.

I do not consider myself a good writer. My communications as a preacher have mostly been verbal. There is a great difference in an oral style and a written style of communications. However, I enjoyed the discipline of writing during the 2022 Lenten season and now have completed these seventy-five devotionals from John's Gospel.

The format of the DAILY DEVOTIONALS is simple. A brief passage of scripture is printed as the scripture reading of the day.

A "THOUGHT FOR THE DAY" is presented.

A "CHALLENGE" is given.

Lastly, a PRAYER is suggested.

The most significant part of the daily devotional is the scripture passage. Thus I have printed the scripture passage for each day. All the scripture passages are from the World English Bible. The reason for using the World English Bible translation, a non copyrighted translation, is that there are no limitations on the amount of scripture that can be printed. I have also found the World English Bible to be a very good and accurate translation. I encourage you to read the passage more than once. Many people find insights by reading additional translations or paraphrases of the passage.

A few of the daily scripture passages are longer that the space available. In order to maintain a uniform style of two pages per day, a few verses are omitted in a few devotionals. In these cases the omission is indicated by ... (ellipsis). I encourage you to read the complete passage from your favorite Bible translation. When additional scripture references are given, look them up and read them.

The "THOUGHT FOR THE DAY" is intentionally brief. It is intended as a "starter" for your response and enlargement. I hope you will be stimulated to think beyond what I have printed. It is not just a thought for the moment. It is intended to be a thought to be reflected on throughout the day.

The "CHALLENGE" is a call for your response to the scripture passage. Reflect/meditate on it. A good discipline would be to write down your initial response at the bottom of the page.

Here are some suggestions for getting the most from your daily scripture/devotional readings:

*Read just one selection a day. Try to focus on the scripture passage/devotional throughout the day. Make the "Challenge" of the day "the meditation of your heart" for the day.

*Use your Bible to read the entire suggested scripture passage and to look up any references given. As mentioned above, to keep the format uniform and brief, a few longer passages are not printed in their entirety.

*Consider reading the scripture passage in a second translation each day.

*Set a specific time each day for your devotional time.

*Share your response with a friend or family member. Doing so will deepen your experience.

DAILY DEVOTIONAL 1

Scripture Reading: John 1:1-18 (World English Bible)

THE WORD BECAME FLESH

1:1 In the beginning was the Word, and the Word was with God, and the Word was God. 2The same was in the beginning with God. 3All things were made through him. Without him was not anything made that has been made. 4In him was life, and the life was the light of men. 5The light shines in the darkness, and the darkness hasn't overcome it.

6There came a man, sent from God, whose name was John. 7The same came as a witness, that he might testify about the light, that all might believe through him. 8He was not the light, but was sent that he might testify about the light. 9The true light that enlightens everyone was coming into the world.

10He was in the world, and the world was made through him, and the world didn't recognize him. 11He came to his own, and those who were his own didn't receive him. 12But as many as received him, to them he gave the right to become God's children, to those who believe in his name: 13who were born not of blood, nor of the will of the flesh, nor of the will of man, but of God.

14The Word became flesh, and lived among us. We saw his glory, such glory as of the one and only Son of the Father, full of grace and truth. 15John testified about him. He cried out, saying, "This was he of whom I said, 'He who comes after me has surpassed me, for he was before me.'" 16From his fullness we all received grace upon grace. 17For the law was given through Moses. Grace and truth were realized through Jesus Christ. 18No one has seen God at any time. The one and only Son, who is in the bosom of the Father, he has declared him.

* * * * * * * * * * * * * *

JIM'S THOUGHT FOR THE DAY

"In the beginning the Word already existed; the Word was with God, and the Word was God." vs. 1

John's Gospel is unique. He does not begin his story of good news with the birth of Jesus at Bethlehem as do Matthew and Luke. He begins in eternity: "In the beginning the Word already existed." vs. 1 (GNT)

WORD is the term for the supreme revelation (expression) of God in Jesus. Think about this amazing truth: God's Son is eternal with God the Father and God the Holy Spirit! "Without Him nothing was made." Our human minds cannot fully comprehend this eternal truth.

"The Word became a human being and, full of grace and truth, lived among us. We saw his glory, the glory which he received as the Father's only Son." vs. 14

Yet we can behold His glory. He has given us the right to be children of God. The song says, "I'm a child of the King."

He was from the very beginning. "And the Word was God." vs. 1

CHALLENGE: *TO KNOW THAT WE ARE KNOW BY GOD IN A PERSONAL WAY AS HIS CHILD AND TO LIVE LIKE IT.*

Prayer:

LORD, Thank you that "I belong to Jesus and Jesus belongs to me. Not for the years of time alone, but for eternity." Amen

DAILY DEVOTIONAL 2

Scripture Reading: John 1:19-34 (World English Bible)

BEHOLD THE LAMB OF GOD

19 This is John's testimony, when the Jews sent priests and Levites from Jerusalem to ask him, "Who are you?"20 He confessed, and didn't deny, but he confessed, "I am not the Christ." 21 They asked him, "What then? Are you Elijah?" He said, "I am not." "Are you the prophet?" He answered, "No."

22 They said therefore to him, "Who are you? Give us an answer to take back to those who sent us. What do you say about yourself? 23 He said, "I am the voice of one crying in the wilderness, 'Make straight the way of the Lord,' as Isaiah the prophet said." 24 The ones who had been sent were from the Pharisees. 25 They asked him, "Why then do you baptize, if you are not the Christ, nor Elijah, nor the Prophet?" 26 John answered them, "I baptize in water, but among you stands one whom you don't know, 27 he who comes after me, whose sandal strap I'm not worthy to untie." 28 These things were done in Bethany beyond the Jordan, where John was baptizing.

29 On the next day, he saw Jesus coming to him, and said, "Behold, the Lamb of God, who takes away the sin of the world! 30 This is he of whom I said, 'After me comes a man who is preferred before me, for he was before me. '31 I didn't know him, but for this reason I came baptizing in water: that he would be revealed to Israel."

32 John testified, saying, "I have seen the Spirit descending like a dove out of heaven, and it remained on him. 33 I didn't recognize him, but he who sent me to baptize in water, he said to me, 'On whoever you will see the Spirit descending, and remaining on him, the same is he who baptizes in the Holy Spirit.' 34 I have seen, and have testified that this is the Son of God."

* * * * * * * * * * * * * *

JIM'S THOUGHT FOR THE DAY

"There is the Lamb of God, who takes away the sin of the world."
vs. 29.

The WORD and the LAMB! John gives us so much to think about.
My mind goes back to the story of Abraham and Isaac in Genesis. When questioned by Isaac about a sacrifice, Abraham answered, "God himself will provide the lamb for the burnt offering, my son." Genesis 22:8

Our journey through the ministry of Jesus with John will reveal how Jesus was and is God's provision for our sins.

"What can wash away my sins?
Nothing but the blood of Jesus!"

"Oh, Lamb of God, I come" just as I am!

CHALLENGE: TO BEHOLD THE LAMB WITH REVERENCE AND AWE AND KNOW THAT HIS BLOOD WAS SHED FOR ME.

Prayer:

LORD, I am not worthy but You are worthy, so I repent and confess my sins today trusting in you alone. Amen

DAILY DEVOTIONAL 3

Scripture Reading: John 1:35-51 (World English Bible)

AND HE BROUGHT HIM TO JESUS

35 Again, the next day, John was standing with two of his disciples, 36 and he looked at Jesus as he walked, and said, "Behold, the Lamb of God!" 37 The two disciples heard him speak, and they followed Jesus. 38 Jesus turned and saw them following, and said to them, "What are you looking for?" They said to him, "Rabbi" (which is to say, being interpreted, Teacher), "where are you staying?"

39 He said to them, "Come and see." They came and saw where he was staying, and they stayed with him that day. It was about the tenth hour.

40 One of the two who heard John and followed him was Andrew, Simon Peter's brother. 41 He first found his own brother, Simon, and said to him, "We have found the Messiah!" (which is, being interpreted, Christ). 42 He brought him to Jesus. Jesus looked at him and said, "You are Simon the son of Jonah. You shall be called Cephas" (which is by interpretation, Peter).

43 On the next day, he was determined to go out into Galilee, and he found Philip. Jesus said to him, "Follow me." 44 Now Philip was from Bethsaida, the city of Andrew and Peter. 45 Philip found Nathanael, and said to him, "We have found him of whom Moses in the law and also the prophets, wrote: Jesus of Nazareth, the son of Joseph."

46 Nathanael said to him, "Can any good thing come out of Nazareth?"

Philip said to him, "Come and see."...(verses 47-51 not printed)

* * * * * * * * * * * * * * * *

JIM'S THOUGHT FOR THE DAY

His name is Andrew. Like most of the disciples we do not know much about him. In this passage John tells us he was the brother of Simon Peter and that he followed Jesus. Then he brought his brother, Simon Peter, to Jesus.

Despite his seemingly important role as an early follower of Christ, Andrew is only mentioned 12 times in the entire New Testament - and four of those times are simply lists of the 12 apostles.

Andrew was the first disciple Jesus called. He along with Phillip brought some Greeks to Jesus. He brought the lad with the loaves and fish to Jesus at the feeding of the 5000. He was the first to declare that Jesus was the Messiah. He is an example for us to follow. He brought people to Jesus.

Do you think of someone who brought you to Jesus?

Who have you brought to Jesus?

CHALLENGE: TO FOLLOW THE EXAMPLE OF ANDREW IN BRINGING PEOPLE TO JESUS.

Prayer:

LORD, open my eyes to people who need you and help me to give a strong and positive witness of your love and grace in my life. Amen

DAILY DEVOTIONAL 4

Scripture Reading: John 2:1-12 (World English Bible)

WHATEVER HE SAYS TO YOU DO IT

2:1 The third day, there was a wedding in Cana of Galilee. Jesus' mother was there. 2 Jesus also was invited, with his disciples, to the wedding. 3 When the wine ran out, Jesus' mother said to him, "They have no wine."4 Jesus said to her, "Woman, what does that have to do with you and me? My hour has not yet come."

5 His mother said to the servants, "Whatever he says to you, do it."

6 Now there were six water pots of stone set there after the Jews' way of purifying, containing two or three metretes apiece. 7 Jesus said to them, "Fill the water pots with water." So they filled them up to the brim. 8 He said to them, "Now draw some out, and take it to the ruler of the feast." So they took it.

9 When the ruler of the feast tasted the water now become wine, and didn't know where it came from (but the servants who had drawn the water knew), the ruler of the feast called the bridegroom 10 and said to him, "Everyone serves the good wine first, and when the guests have drunk freely, then that which is worse. You have kept the good wine until now!"

11 This beginning of his signs Jesus did in Cana of Galilee, and revealed his glory; and his disciples believed in him.
12 After this, he went down to Capernaum, he, and his mother, his brothers, and his disciples; and they stayed there a few days.

* * * * * * * * * * * * * * * *

JIM'S THOUGHT FOR THE DAY

Mary said, "Whatever he says to you, do it". vs. 5

John records Jesus' first miracle (he calls them "signs" vs. 11.) Several phrases in this passage jump out at me.

"Why do you involve me?" vs. 4
"You have saved the best until now." vs. 10
"His disciples believed in him." vs. 11

But the most striking phrase to me are the words of Mary, "Whatever he says to you, do it." vs. 5

Obedience is an essential part of faith. The gospel song gives us a good definition of faith: "Trust and Obey." The factor of obedience in faith will be seen throughout John's Gospel.

What step of obedience do you need to take today? Listen. Respond. Do it!

CHALLENGE: TO SEEK TO UNDERSTAND HIS WILL AND TO DO WHAT JESUS TELLS ME TO DO.

Prayer:

LORD, Give me obedience even when I do not fully understand. Amen

DAILY DEVOTIONAL 5

John 2:13-22 (WEB)

BELIEVE THE SCRIPTURES

Jesus Clears the Temple

2:13 The Passover of the Jews was at hand, and Jesus went up to Jerusalem.

14 He found in the temple those who sold oxen, sheep, and doves, and the changers of money sitting.

15 He made a whip of cords, and threw all out of the temple, both the sheep and the oxen; and he poured out the changers' money, and overthrew their tables.

16 To those who sold the doves, he said, "Take these things out of here! Don't make my Father's house a marketplace!"

17 His disciples remembered that it was written, "Zeal for your house will eat me up." {Psalm 69:9}

18 The Jews therefore answered him, "What sign do you show us, seeing that you do these things?"

19 Jesus answered them, "Destroy this temple, and in three days I will raise it up."

20 The Jews therefore said, "Forty-six years was this temple in building, and will you raise it up in three days?"

21 But he spoke of the temple of his body.

22 When therefore he was raised from the dead, his disciples remembered that he said this, and they believed the Scripture, and the word which Jesus had said.

* *

JIM'S THOUGHT FOR THE DAY

" ... and they believed the scripture and what Jesus had said." vs. 22

John records that Jesus cleansed the temple early in his ministry as recorded here. John also records that Jesus once again cleansed the temple at the end of his ministry.

I can only hope that your experience in God's house of worship has been as uplifting and positive as mine. I want my devotion to God's house to "burn in me like a fire."

Jesus was upset that the Temple had been turned into a marketplace.
It is easy for the sacred to become secular. You and I need to keep God's house above reproach and free of materialism and greed.

And we must believe the scriptures. Again notice the theme of "believe". We will continue to follow this theme of John's Gospel. The first disciples believed. Those at the wedding in Cana believed. Nicodemus believed. The woman at the well believed. The temple official believed. The lame man believed. The 5000 believed.

CHALLENGE: TO BELIEVE WITH A RESPONSE OF OBEDIENCE THAT CHANGES ME. BELIEVE!

Prayer:

LORD, I want to be a part of what you are doing in my world. I want to be an example of believing. Amen

DAILY DEVOTIONAL 6

Scripture Reading: John 3:1-16 (WEB)

LIFE AT IT'S BEST IS NOT GOOD ENOUGH

Jesus Teaches Nicodemus

3 Now there was a Pharisee, a man named Nicodemus who was a member of the Jewish ruling council. 2 He came to Jesus at night and said, "Rabbi, we know that you are a teacher who has come from God. For no one could perform the signs you are doing if God were not with him."3 Jesus replied, "Very truly I tell you, no one can see the kingdom of God unless they are born again."

4 "How can someone be born when they are old?" Nicodemus asked. "Surely they cannot enter a second time into their mother's womb to be born!"5 Jesus answered, "Very truly I tell you, no one can enter the kingdom of God unless they are born of water and the Spirit. 6 Flesh gives birth to flesh, but the Spirit gives birth to spirit. 7 You should not be surprised at my saying, 'You must be born again.'

8 The wind blows wherever it pleases. You hear its sound, but you cannot tell where it comes from or where it is going. So it is with everyone born of the Spirit." 9 "How can this be?" Nicodemus asked.10 "You are Israel's teacher," said Jesus, "and do you not understand these things? ...

14 Just as Moses lifted up the snake in the wilderness, so the Son of Man must be lifted up, 15 that everyone who believes may need have eternal life in him."16 For God so loved the world that he gave his one and only Son, that whoever believes in him shall not perish but have eternal life.

* *

14

JIM'S THOUGHT FOR THE DAY

"There was a Jewish leader named Nicodemus ..." vs. 3

Nicodemus was a good man. He was religious. He was righteous. He kept the law. He was morally upright. But Nicodemus is an example THAT LIFE AT ITS BEST IS NOT GOOD ENOUGH.

He knew something was missing. That is why he came to Jesus one night. Did he come at night so as not to be seen? Not necessarily. Let's give him the benefit of the doubt. He came seeking spiritual answers. And Jesus gave him answers. "You must be born again." Birth is both physical and spiritual. Those only born physically die twice - physically and spiritually. Those born physically and spiritually only die once. Jesus promised, "Whoever lives and believes in me will never die." John 11:26

John 3:16 has been called "the gospel in a nutshell." I substitute my name for "the world" - "God so loved Jim McCluskey that he gave his one and only Son ...". Put your name in the verse.

Jesus' reference to the serpents in the wilderness (vs. 14) is a reminder of God's eternal plan for our receiving eternal life. Numbers 21

Nicodemus became an open follower of Jesus. After the crucifixion he brought spices to anoint the body of Jesus. (John 19:39)

Life at its best is not good enough, but Jesus is good enough!

CHALLENGE: TO CONFESS THAT MY "RIGHTEOUS IS LIKE FILTHY RAGS" AND MY ONLY HOPE FOR ETERNAL LIFE IS IN JESUS.

Prayer:

LORD, May my new life in You be a shining light in a dark world. Thank you. Amen

DAILY DEVOTIONAL 7

Scripture Reading: John 3:17-21 (WEB)

LIGHT HAS COME INTO THE WORLD

3:17 For God did not send his Son into the world to condemn the world, but to save the world through him. 18 Whoever believes in him is not condemned, but whoever does not believe stands condemned because they have not believed in the name of God's one and only Son.

19 This is the verdict: Light has come into the world, but people loved darkness instead of light because their deeds were evil. 20 Everyone who does evil hates the light, and will not come into the light for fear that their deeds will be exposed. 21 But whoever lives by the truth comes into the light, so that it may be seen plainly that what they have done has been done in the sight of God.

John 3:17-21 (Good News Translation)
3:17 For God did not send his Son into the world to be its judge, but to be its savior.
18 Those who believe in the Son are not judged; but those who do not believe have already been judged, because they have not believed in God's only Son.

19 This is how the judgment works: the light has come into the world, but people love the darkness rather than the light, because their deeds are evil. 20 Those who do evil things hate the light and will not come to the light, because they do not want their evil deeds to be shown up. 21 But those who do what is true come to the light in order that the light may show that what they did was in obedience to God.

* * * * * * * * * * * * * * * *

JIM'S THOUGHT FOR THE DAY

"The light has come into the world" vs. 19
Lighthouses have become historic relics. They still have a charm. But once their function was necessary for naval safety. The imagery of the lighthouse is used in many gospel songs. One of my favorites:

"... I thank God for the lighthouse
I owe my life to Him
Jesus is the lighthouse
And from the rocks of sin
He has shown a light around me
That I might clearly see
If it wasn't for the lighthouse
Tell me where would this ship be?"

Jesus brings light. Light brings vision. It brings understanding. Light gives direction. Light reveals. Light brings safety. Light drives out darkness.

Jesus: the Light of the World! The Light has come!

CHALLENGE: TO WALK IN HIS LIGHT AND TO REFUSE TO LIVE IN DARKNESS.

Prayer:

LORD, I want to keep my eyes focused on you. Shine the light of truth on me. Expose my sin. Light up my paths.

DAILY DEVOTIONAL 8

Scripture Reading: John 3:22-30 (WEB)

HE MUST INCREASE. I MUST DECREASE.

22After these things, Jesus came with his disciples into the land of Judea. He stayed there with them, and baptized. 23John also was baptizing in Enon near Salim, because there was much water there. They came, and were baptized. 24For John was not yet thrown into prison.

25There arose therefore a questioning on the part of John's disciples with some Jews about purification. 26They came to John, and said to him, "Rabbi, he who was with you beyond the Jordan, to whom you have testified, behold, the same baptizes, and everyone is coming to him."

27John answered, "A man can receive nothing, unless it has been given him from heaven. 28You yourselves testify that I said, 'I am not the Christ,' but, 'I have been sent before him.' 29He who has the bride is the bridegroom; but the friend of the bridegroom, who stands and hears him, rejoices greatly because of the bridegroom's voice. This, my joy, therefore is made full.

30He must increase, but I must decrease.

* * * * * * * * * * * * * * * *

JIM'S THOUGHT FOR THE DAY

"He must increase, but I must decrease. "

John knew his place. He fulfilled his role. He accepted God's plan.

That was not easy. And it is not easy for you or me. Accepting God's plan is all important. We are tempted to feel self reliant. My way or God's way? The battle continues. Remember the commitment of John the Baptist: "He must increase, but I must decrease."

Simply said: "Jesus first."

Years ago we had two "revivals" a year. The response of the congregation to the preacher of the week was always interesting. Sometimes people would say: "Isn't the preacher wonderful?" Other times they would say: "Isn't Jesus wonderful?" There is a big difference.

Do you put Jesus first?

CHALLENGE: TO ALWAYS PUT JESUS FIRST IN MY WORDS AND IN LIFE. TO FIND AND FULFILL GOD'S PURPOSE FOR MY LIFE.

Prayer:

LORD, Help me to always put you first in my life.

DAILY DEVOTIONAL 9

Scripture Reading: John 3:31-36 (WEB)

TRUST AND OBEY

The Father loves His Son

31He who comes from above is above all. He who is from the earth belongs to the earth, and speaks of the earth. He who comes from heaven is above all. 32What he has seen and heard, of that he testifies; and no one receives his witness. 33He who has received his witness has set his seal to this, that God is true. 34For he whom God has sent speaks the words of God; for God gives the Spirit without measure.

35The Father loves the Son, and has given all things into his hand. 36One who believes in the Son has eternal life, but one who disobeys the Son won't see life, but the wrath of God remains on him."

John 3:31-36 (GNT)

3:31 He who comes from above is greater than all. He who is from the earth belongs to the earth and speaks about earthly matters, but he who comes from heaven is above all. 32 He tells what he has seen and heard, yet no one accepts his message. 33 But whoever accepts his message confirms by this that God is truthful. 34 The one whom God has sent speaks God's words, because God gives him the fullness of his Spirit.

35 The Father loves his Son and has put everything in his power. 36 Whoever believes in the Son has eternal life; whoever disobeys the Son will not have life, but will remain under God's punishment.

* *

JIM'S THOUGHT FOR THE DAY

What is the opposite of faith? The usual response is doubt. But according to verse 36 the opposite of faith is disobedience. We are commanded to believe.

Obedience is defined as "submission to another's authority." Synonyms are compliance, conformity, submission, subordination

Disobedience is "Neglect or refusal to obey; violation of a command or prohibition; the omission of that which is commanded to be done, or the doing of that which is forbid."

Repeatedly Jesus calls for our obedience. Remember that obedience is an essential part of faith.

Again I am reminded that a good definition of New Testament faith is in the gospel song title "Trust and Obey".

Are you an obedient follower of Jesus?

CHALLENGE: *TO HAVE A FAITH THAT INCLUDED COMPLETE OBEDIENCE TO GOD'S WILL FOR MY LIFE.*

Prayer:

LORD, Help me to seek and discern your will so I can be pleasing in your sight. Amen.

DAILY DEVOTIONAL 10

Scripture Reading: John 4:1-15 (WEB)

LIFE AT ITS BEST IS NOT GOOD ENOUGH

1.... 4 He needed to pass through Samaria.5So he came to a city of Samaria, called Sychar, near the parcel of ground that Jacob gave to his son, Joseph.6 Jacob's well was there. Jesus therefore, being tired from his journey, sat down by the well. It was about the sixth hour. 7A woman of Samaria came to draw water. Jesus said to her, "Give me a drink."8 For his disciples had gone away into the city to buy food.

9 The Samaritan woman therefore said to him, "How is it that you, being a Jew, ask for a drink from me, a Samaritan woman?" (For Jews have no dealings with Samaritans.)

10 Jesus answered her, "If you knew the gift of God, and who it is who says to you, 'Give me a drink,' you would have asked him, and he would have given you living water."

11 The woman said to him, "Sir, you have nothing to draw with, and the well is deep. From where then have you that living water?

12 Are you greater than our father, Jacob, who gave us the well, and drank of it himself, as did his sons, and his cattle?"

13 Jesus answered her, "Everyone who drinks of this water will thirst again, 14but whoever drinks of the water that I will give him will never thirst; but the water that I will give him will become in him a well of water springing up to eternal life."

15 The woman said to him, "Sir, give me this water, so that I don't get thirsty, neither come all the way here to draw.

* * * * * * * * * * * * * * * * * *

JIM'S THOUGHT FOR THE DAY

"...whoever drinks of the water that I will give him will never thirst" vs. 14

First, I want us to think about this woman. Her life was a mess. She was a "sinful woman". She was probably drawing water in the middle of the day because she was not welcomed there by her neighbors because of her bad reputation and character.

She needed living water that gives eternal satisfaction. Water is essential for life. Water is mentioned a total of 722 times in the Bible, more often than faith, hope, prayer, and worship. In spiritual use, water represents the thirst of the soul for God. "He leads me to still waters. He restores my soul." Psalm 23:2,3

Nicodemus is a reminder that LIFE AT ITS BEST IS NOT GOOD ENOUGH. This Samaritan woman is a reminder that LIFE AT ITS WORST IS NOT WITHOUT HOPE.

Ever felt unforgivable? I think this woman did. Well, she was not and you are not. Jesus loves you regardless of anything you have ever done. He will forgive you no matter what. Just ask him!

CHALLENGE: TO ACCEPT THE TRUTH THAT I AM A SINNER SAVED BY GRACE, UNWORTHY OF HIS LOVE BUT LOVED BY JESUS.

Prayer:

LORD, I need what only you can give: Forgiveness. Jesus I come to you. Give me living water.

DAILY DEVOTIONAL 11

Scripture Reading: John 4:16-26 (WEB)

WORSHIP IN SPIRIT AND TRUTH

16Jesus said to her, "Go, call your husband, and come here."

17The woman answered, "I have no husband."
Jesus said to her, "You said well, 'I have no husband,' 18for you have had five husbands; and he whom you now have is not your husband. This you have said truly."

19The woman said to him, "Sir, I perceive that you are a prophet. 20Our fathers worshiped in this mountain, and you Jews say that in Jerusalem is the place where people ought to worship."

21Jesus said to her, "Woman, believe me, the hour comes, when neither in this mountain, nor in Jerusalem, will you worship the Father. 22You worship that which you don't know. We worship that which we know; for salvation is from the Jews. 23But the hour comes, and now is, when the true worshipers will worship the Father in spirit and truth, for the Father seeks such to be his worshipers. 24God is spirit, and those who worship him must worship in spirit and truth."

25The woman said to him, "I know that Messiah comes, he who is called Christ. When he has come, he will declare to us all things."

26Jesus said to her, "I am he, the one who speaks to you."

* * * * * * * * * * * * * * * * *

JIM'S THOUGHT OF THE DAY

"... worship the Father in Spirit and in Truth... vs. 23

This passage is a continuation of the conversation between the Samaritan woman at the well of Jacob and Jesus.

Jesus asks the woman about her husband. Obviously Jesus already knew her story. Why then did he ask? The answer is in his desire for her to truly receive the water of life she had asked for.

Her bringing up the proper place to worship was an attempt to divert the conversation away from her sinful past. Jesus uses the opportunity to help her understand that true worship is not about a place but is about spirit and truth. It is yet another way Jesus teaches us about himself and our relationship with him. We are challenged to accept the Truth with a spirit of surrender.

CHALLENGE: TO WORSHIP JESUS WITH A SPIRIT OF OBEDIENT FAITH LED BY HIS SPIRIT.

Prayer:

LORD, Help my worship of you to be genuine and whole knowing you are the Messiah who knows all about us but loves us anyway. Amen.

DAILY DEVOTIONAL 12

Scripture Reading: John 4:27-38 (WEB)

YOUR BIGGEST CRAVING

4:27At this his disciples came. They marveled that he was speaking with a woman; yet no one said, "What are you looking for?" or, "Why do you speak with her?

28So the woman left her water pot, and went away into the city, and said to the people, 29"Come, see a man who told me everything that I did. Can this be the Christ?"

30They went out of the city, and were coming to him. 31In the meanwhile, the disciples urged him, saying, "Rabbi, eat."

32But he said to them, "I have food to eat that you don't know about."33The disciples therefore said to one another, "Has anyone brought him something to eat?"

34Jesus said to them, "My food is to do the will of him who sent me, and to accomplish his work. 35Don't you say, 'There are yet four months until the harvest?' Behold, I tell you, lift up your eyes, and look at the fields, that they are white for harvest already. 36He who reaps receives wages, and gathers fruit to eternal life; that both he who sows and he who reaps may rejoice together.

37For in this the saying is true, 'One sows, and another reaps.' 38I sent you to reap that for which you haven't labored. Others have labored, and you have entered into their labor."

* * * * * * * * * * * * * * * * * * *

JIM'S THOUGHT FOR THE DAY

"My food is to obey the will of the one who sent me…" vs. 34 (GNT)

There it is again: obey! The desire of the life of Jesus was to obey the Father. That was the nourishment he needed and desired. John just keeps this theme alive: OBEY!

What do you crave? What is the biggest desire of your life? Most often our desires are self centered. We want what we think will please and satisfy us. But on achieving our desires and wants we are left thirsty and hungry and not satisfied.

Jesus finished the work God the Father gave him to do. We are to follow his example.

Obeying God brings satisfaction.
Obeying God brings forgiveness.
Obeying God brings happiness.
Obeying God brings fulfillment.
Obeying God brings blessings.
Obeying God brings everlasting life.

CHALLENGE: TO DESIRE ABOVE ALL ELSE TO DO AND FINISH THE WORK GOD GAVE ME TO DO.

Prayer:

LORD, Help me to find and do your will. Amen

DAILY DEVOTIONAL 13

Scripture Reading: John 4:39-42 (WEB)

BELIEVE HAVING HEARD FOR YOURSELF

39From that city many of the Samaritans believed in him because of the word of the woman, who testified, "He told me everything that I did." 40So when the Samaritans came to him, they begged him to stay with them. He stayed there two days.

41Many more believed because of his word.

42They said to the woman, "Now we believe, not because of your speaking; for we have heard for ourselves, and know that this is indeed the Christ, the Savior of the world."

John 4:39-43 (GNT)
39 Many of the Samaritans in that town believed in Jesus because the woman had said, "He told me everything I have ever done." 40 So when the Samaritans came to him, they begged him to stay with them, and Jesus stayed there two days.

41 Many more believed because of his message,

42 and they told the woman, "We believe now, not because of what you said, but because we ourselves have heard him, and we know that he really is the Savior of the world."

* * * * * * * * * * * * * * * *

JIM'S THOUGHT FOR THE DAY

"Now we believe, not because of your speaking; for we have heard for ourselves, and know that this is indeed the Christ, the Savior of the world." vs. 42

A familiar hymn is, "Faith of our Fathers". We should be thankful for a heritage of faith. Many of you, like me, were brought up in a Christian home with parents of faith. As such we have been blessed.

But our faith must be personal. We cannot rest in the faith of anyone else. The family and acquaintances of the Samaritan woman came to believe in Jesus not just because she believed but "because we ourselves have heard him, and we know that he really is the Savior of the world." vs. 42

I am thankful for my Christian heritage. But one day I came to know myself that Jesus is the savior of the world and my personal savior.

Aren't you glad that you are included in "whosoever believes in him shall not perish but have everlasting life."

CHALLENGE: TO KEEP MY RELATIONSHIP WITH GOD VERY PERSONAL BY DAILY COMMITMENT AND PRAYER.

Prayer:

LORD, I desire fellowship with you and am thankful for who you are as my Heavenly Father. Amen.

DAILY DEVOTIONAL 14

Scripture Reading: John 4:43-54 (WEB)

THE SIGNS OF JESUS

43After the two days he went out from there and went into Galilee. 44For Jesus himself testified that a prophet has no honor in his own country. 45So when he came into Galilee, the Galileans received him, having seen all the things that he did in Jerusalem at the feast, for they also went to the feast.

46Jesus came therefore again to Cana of Galilee, where he made the water into wine. There was a certain nobleman whose son was sick at Capernaum. 47When he heard that Jesus had come out of Judea into Galilee, he went to him, and begged him that he would come down and heal his son, for he was at the point of death. 48Jesus therefore said to him, "Unless you see signs and wonders, you will in no way believe."

49The nobleman said to him, "Sir, come down before my child dies." 50Jesus said to him, "Go your way. Your son lives." The man believed the word that Jesus spoke to him, and he went his way. 51As he was now going down, his servants met him and reported, saying "Your child lives!" 52So he inquired of them the hour when he began to get better. They said therefore to him, "Yesterday at the seventh hour, the fever left him." 53So the father knew that it was at that hour in which Jesus said to him, "Your son lives." He believed, as did his whole house. 54This is again the second sign that Jesus did, having come out of Judea into Galilee.

* * * * * * * * * * * * * * * *

JIM'S THOUGHT FOR THE DAY

John records several acts of Jesus that are not recorded in the other gospels. John does not call them miracles, he calls them "signs". John interpreted them to be more than miracles. They were events that pointed to the power of God through his son Jesus. The signs are illustrations of spiritual truths shown by these acts of Jesus.

John gives us seven signs in his gospel. The first sign is the turning of water into wine (John 2). The second is in this passage: the healing of the nobleman's son. In all, John gives us seven signs. Seven is a number that represents completeness or wholeness. We will look for the other five sign later in the gospel.

The faith of the nobleman (or public official) is complete and whole. He did not insist that Jesus go to his home in Capernaum to visit his sick son. He believed the word of Jesus that his son would live. He and his family believed.

I believe God still gives signs: evidences of his presence and work. We are sometimes called upon just to believe. "Lord, I believe. Help my unbelief." Mark 9:24

CHALLENGE: TO HAVE A TRUSTING FAITH THAT OVERCOMES DOUBT.

Prayer:

LORD, Help me to have a trusting faith that takes your promises as true. Amen

DAILY DEVOTIONAL 15

Scripture Reading: John 5:1-15 (WEB)

DO YOU WANT TO BE MADE WELL?

Jesus Heals at the Pool of Bethesda
1After these things, there was a feast of the Jews, and Jesus went up to Jerusalem.2Now in Jerusalem by the sheep gate, there is a pool, which is called in Hebrew, "Bethesda," having five porches. 3In these lay a great multitude of those who were sick, blind, lame, or paralyzed, waiting for the moving of the water; 4for an angel went down at certain times into the pool, and stirred up the water. Whoever stepped in first after the stirring of the water was made whole of whatever disease he had. 5A certain man was there, who had been sick for thirty-eight years. 6When Jesus saw him lying there, and knew that he had been sick for a long time, he asked him, "Do you want to be made well?" 7The sick man answered him, "Sir, I have no one to put me into the pool when the water is stirred up, but while I'm coming, another steps down before me."
8Jesus said to him, "Arise, take up your mat, and walk." 9Immediately, the man was made well, and took up his mat and walked. Now it was the Sabbath on that day.

10So the Jews said to him who was cured, "It is the Sabbath. It is not lawful for you to carry the mat." 11He answered them, "He who made me well, the same said to me, 'Take up your mat, and walk.'" 12Then they asked him, "Who is the man who said to you, 'Take up your mat, and walk'?" 13But he who was healed didn't know who it was, for Jesus had withdrawn, a crowd being in the place. 14Afterward Jesus found him in the temple, and said to him, "Behold, you are made well. Sin no more, so that nothing worse happens to you."
15The man went away, and told the Jews that it was Jesus who had made him well.

* * * * * * * * * * * * * *

JIM'S THOUGHT FOR THE DAY

"Take up your mat and walk." For 38 years this poor man had longed and waited for healing. I wonder why he had not given up years before.

This event took place at the pool of Bethesda. Bethesda means "house of mercy." It certainly became a house of mercy for this sick man. Jesus made him well and whole. With a simple word Jesus made it possible for him to "take up his mat and walk".

Jesus asks him what seems to be a strange question: "Do you want to be made well?" I am not sure I know the answer as to why. I do know that I have seen many people miserable in their sins who were not trying to change their lives.

Sometimes faith comes after God intervene. Sometimes before. This is another time I wish I knew the rest of the story!

A friend told me an amazing story of a badly crippled child who was helped by a charity for handicapped children and make able to walk and run. He asks me, "Do you know where he is today? He is in prison. We taught him how to walk but not where to walk!"

Jesus teaches us where to walk. "Behold you are made well. Sin no more." vs. 14

CHALLENGE: TO HAVE THE DESIRE TO BE LIKE JESUS IN MY CONDUCT AND SERVICE.

Prayer:

LORD: Make my life a blessing that reflects my thankfulness and appreciation for your healing in my life. Amen

DAILY DEVOTIONAL 16

Scripture Reading: John 5:16-23 (WEB)

LIKE FATHER, LIKE SON

16For this cause the Jews persecuted Jesus, and sought to kill him, because he did these things on the Sabbath. 17But Jesus answered them, "My Father is still working, so I am working, too."

18For this cause therefore the Jews sought all the more to kill him, because he not only broke the Sabbath, but also called God his own Father, making himself equal with God.

19Jesus therefore answered them, "Most certainly, I tell you, the Son can do nothing of himself, but what he sees the Father doing. For whatever things he does, these the Son also does likewise.

20For the Father has affection for the Son, and shows him all things that he himself does. He will show him greater works than these, that you may marvel.

21For as the Father raises the dead and gives them life, even so the Son also gives life to whom he desires.

22For the Father judges no one, but he has given all judgment to the Son, 23that all may honor the Son, even as they honor the Father.

He who doesn't honor the Son doesn't honor the Father who sent him.

* * * * * * * * * * * * * * * * *

JIM'S THOUGHT FOR THE DAY

Which is true? Jesus is like God; or God is like Jesus? The answer is "both/and". God the Father and God the Son are one. "I and the Father are one." John 10:30. All of the characteristics and attributes of each one belong to the other.

However, the coming of Jesus into our world as a historical figure was for the purpose of revealing the full nature of the Heavenly Father to us.

Remember John's prologue: "The Word became flesh, and lived among us. We saw his glory, such glory as of the one and only Son of the Father, full of grace and truth." John 1:14.

Jesus always did what the Father wanted him to do. As Jesus is to His Father, so we must be to Jesus. This is an obedience based on faith and love.

CHALLENGE: TO FOLLOW THE EXAMPLE OF JESUS IN DOING THE WILL OF GOD IN OUR LIVES.

Prayer:

LORD: "Let the words of my mouth and the meditation of my heart be acceptable in your sight". Psalm 19:14 Amen

DAILY DEVOTIONAL 17

Scripture Reading: John 5:23-30

DEAD OR ALIVE

23 Most certainly I tell you, he who hears my word, and believes him who sent me, has eternal life, and doesn't come into judgment, but has passed out of death into life.

25Most certainly, I tell you, the hour comes, and now is, when the dead will hear the Son of God's voice; and those who hear will live.

26For as the Father has life in himself, even so he gave to the Son also to have life in himself. 27He also gave him authority to execute judgment, because he is a son of man.

28Don't marvel at this, for the hour comes, in which all that are in the tombs will hear his voice, 29and will come out; those who have done good, to the resurrection of life; and those who have done evil, to the resurrection of judgment.

30I can of myself do nothing. As I hear, I judge, and my judgment is righteous; because I don't seek my own will, but the will of my Father who sent me.

* * * * * * * * * * * * * * * *

JIM'S THOUGHT FOR THE DAY

Jesus is the life-giver and the life-bringer.

The word "dead" is used in this passage in two ways. First, it is used of those who are spiritually dead. The wages of sin is death. Jesus came to give life, eternal life, to those dead in their trespasses and sins. The word is also used of physical death.

Are you dead or alive? Jesus says in John 14:25, 26. "I am the resurrection and the life. He who believes in me will still live, even if he dies. Whoever lives and believes in me will never die."

I repeat: Once born men die twice. Twice born men only die once. We are told we must be born of the flesh and of the spirit. Each of us makes a choice about our eternal life.

Choose life!

CHALLENGE: TO HAVE THE ASSURANCE OF ETERNAL LIFE THROUGH JESUS CHRIST GOD'S SON.

Prayer:

LORD, Thank you for being the life-giver to my life; for grace that is greater than all my sins. Amen.

DAILY DEVOTIONAL 18

Scripture Reading: John 5:31-47 (WEB)

WITNESSES TO JESUS

31"If I testify about myself, my witness is not valid. 32It is another who testifies about me. I know that the testimony which he testifies about me is true 33You have sent to John, and he has testified to the truth. 34But the testimony which I receive is not from man. However, I say these things that you may be saved. 35He was the burning and shining lamp, and no you were willing to rejoice for a while in his light.

36But the testimony which I have is greater than that of John, for the works which the Father gave me to accomplish, the very works that I do, testify about me, that the Father has sent me. 37The Father himself, who sent me, has testified about me. You have neither heard his voice at any time, nor seen his form. 38You don't have his word living in you; because you don't believe him whom he sent.

39"You search the Scriptures, because you think that in them you have eternal life; and these are they which testify about me. 40Yet you will not come to me, that you may have life. 41I don't receive glory from men. 42But I know you, that you don't have God's love in yourselves. 43I have come in my Father's name, and you don't receive me. If another comes in his own name, you will receive him. 44How can you believe, who receive glory from one another, and you don't seek the glory that comes from the only God? 45"Don't think that I will accuse you to the Father.

There is one who accuses you, even Moses, on whom you have set your hope. 46For if you believed Moses, you would believe me; for he wrote about me. 47But if you don't believe his writings, how will you believe my words

* * * * * * * * * * * * * * * * *

JIM'S THOUGHT FOR THE DAY

The ultimate question is: Who is Jesus?

The religious authorities were offended that Jesus said he was one with God the Father. To them that was blasphemy! It was because of that that they began to plot the death of Jesus.

In answering their questions about what right he had to claim he was one with God, Jesus gives three witnesses. But first he acknowledges that a person cannot just witness to himself. vs. 31

First, Jesus states the witness of John the Baptist. vs. 33. John testified on his behalf.

Second, the Father gives witness to him. "And the Father, who sent me, also testifies on my behalf." vs. 37

Third, the scriptures give witness as to who he is. "And these very Scriptures speak about me!" vs. 39. He goes on to quote the authority of Moses. "If you had really believed Moses, you would have believed me, because he wrote about me." vs. 46

Jesus would later ask Simon Peter, "But who do you say that I am?"

Are you a witness to who Jesus is? Does your life honor him as the divine Son of God?

Well, who do you say he is?

CHALLENGE: TO CONFESS THAT JESUS IS LORD TO THE GLORY OF GOD THE FATHER.

Prayer:

LORD, Help me to witness in word and deed that Jesus is the Christ, the Son of the Living God. Amen.

DAILY DEVOTIONAL 19

Scripture Reading: John 6:1-15 (WEB)

THE ALL-SUFFICIENT LORD

6:1. After these things, Jesus went away to the other side of the Sea of Galilee, which is also called the Sea of Tiberias.

2. A great multitude followed him, because they saw his signs which he did on those who were sick.

3. Jesus went up into the mountain, and he sat there with his disciples. 4. Now the Passover, the feast of the Jews, was at hand.

5. Jesus therefore lifting up his eyes, and seeing that a great multitude was coming to him, said to Philip, "Where are we to buy bread, that these may eat?"

6. This he said to test him, for he himself knew what he would do.

7. Philip answered him, "Two hundred denarii worth of bread is not sufficient for them, that everyone of them may receive a little."

8. One of his disciples, Andrew, Simon Peter's brother, said to him,

9. "There is a boy here who has five barley loaves and two fish, but what are these among so many?" 10. Jesus said, "Have the people sit down." Now there was much grass in that place. So the men sat down, in number about five thousand.

11. Jesus took the loaves; and having given thanks, he distributed to the disciples, and the disciples to those who were sitting down; likewise also of the fish as much as they desired.

12. When they were filled, he said to his disciples, "Gather up the broken pieces which are left over, that nothing be lost."

13. So they gathered them up, and filled twelve baskets with broken pieces from the five barley loaves, which were left over by those who had eaten.

14. When therefore the people saw the sign which Jesus did, they said, "This is truly the prophet who comes into the world." ...

* * * * * * * * * * * * * * * *

JIM'S THOUGHT FOR THE DAY

We meet Andrew again. Remember that he was the first disciple Jesus called. And the first thing he did was bring his brother Simon Peter to Jesus. Again we find him bringing someone to Jesus.

This time it was a boy who had five barley loaves and three fish. What Jesus would do with that boy's small lunch would amaze the world. None of this would have happened if Andrew had not brought the boy to Jesus. Be an Andrew! Bring people to Jesus.

And the boy is an eternal example of what Jesus can do with what we give to him even if it seems so small. Sometimes we all feel so small and insignificant. What we have to offer seems it would not matter.

But Jesus is the great multiplier. He can take our little and make it much. You and I are not insignificant in God's plan. What we have to give is not unimportant.

This is John's fourth "sign". Signs point beyond themselves both to confirm Jesus' identity as the Son of God and to reveal the invisible Father through the actions of his Son.

CHALLENGE: TO FIND OUR OPPORTUNITIES TO BRING OTHERS TO JESUS AND TO GIVE WHAT WE HAVE TO JESUS.

Prayer:

LORD, Give me spiritual insights to see and use opportunities to meet people and their needs. Amen.

DAILY DEVOTIONAL 20

Scripture Reading: John 6:16-24

THE PRESENCE OF JESUS

6:16. When evening came, his disciples went down to the sea,
17. and they entered into the boat, and were going over the sea to Capernaum. It was now dark, and Jesus had not come to them.

18. The sea was tossed by a great wind blowing.

19. When therefore they had rowed about twenty-five or thirty stadia, they saw Jesus walking on the sea, and drawing near to the boat; and they were afraid.

20. But he said to them, "It is I. Don't be afraid."

21. They were willing therefore to receive him into the boat. Immediately the boat was at the land where they were going.

22. On the next day, the multitude that stood on the other side of the sea saw that there was no other boat there, except the one in which his disciples had embarked, and that Jesus hadn't entered with his disciples into the boat, but his disciples had gone away alone.

23. However boats from Tiberias came near to the place where they ate the bread after the Lord had given thanks.24. When the multitude therefore saw that Jesus wasn't there, nor his disciples, they themselves got into the boats, and came to Capernaum, seeking Jesus.

* * * * * * * * * * * * * *

JIM'S THOUGHT FOR THE DAY

"But he said to them, "It is I. Don't be afraid." vs. 20

It was a dark stormy night on the Sea of Galilee. The disciples were alone in the small fishing boat. They had good reason to be afraid. "The sea was tossed by a great wind blowing." I expect more than one of them had expressed that they wished Jesus was with them.

Then just at the time of their need Jesus comes to them walking on the water. He assures them, "It is I. Don't be afraid."

The presence of Jesus brought the disciples safety and encouragement. His promise to us is to be with us always. The gospel song says:

"I've seen the lightning flashing, And heard the thunder roll,
I've felt sin's breakers dashing, trying to conquer my soul;
I've heard the voice of my Savior, He bid me still fight on:
He promised never to leave me, Never to leave me alone."

This is the fifth "sign" in the gospel of John. Remember a sign gives spiritual truth about the Son of God. This was more than a one-time miracle. It is a continuing promise to you and me.

Are you feeling alone? Remember the assurance: "Even though I walk through the valley of the shadow of death, I will fear no evil, for you are with me." Psalm 23:4

CHALLENGE: TO RECOGNIZE THE EVER PRESENCE OF JESUS IN MY LIFE.

Prayer:

LORD, I do not want to live my life in fear. I want your peace that passes all understanding. Amen

DAILY DEVOTIONAL 21

Scripture Reading: John 6:25-34

DOING THE WORK OF GOD: BELIEVE

25 When they found him on the other side of the sea, they asked him, "Rabbi, when did you come here?"
26 Jesus answered them, "Most certainly I tell you, you seek me, not because you saw signs, but because you ate of the loaves, and were filled. 27 Don't work for the food which perishes, but for the food which remains to eternal life, which the Son of Man will give to you. For God the Father has sealed him."

28 They said therefore to him, "What must we do, that we may work the works of God?"
29 Jesus answered them, "This is the work of God, that you believe in him whom he has sent."

30 They said therefore to him, "What then do you do for a sign, that we may see and believe you? What work do you do? 31 Our fathers ate the manna in the wilderness. As it is written, 'He gave them bread out of heaven to eat.'"

32 Jesus therefore said to them, "Most certainly, I tell you, it wasn't Moses who gave you the bread out of heaven, but my Father gives you the true bread out of heaven. 33 For the bread of God is that which comes down out of heaven, and gives life to the world."

34 They said therefore to him, "Lord, always give us this bread."

* * * * * * * * * * * * * *

JIM'S THOUGHT FOR THE DAY

"Jesus answered them, "This is the work of God, that you believe in him whom he has sent." vs. 29

The first step in following Jesus is to believe in him. We are tempted to do other things first.
* Some feel like they need to straighten up their lives before they come to Jesus.
* Others feel the must do some good works first in order to deserve eternal life.
* Still others seek a relationship to the church first before believing.
* Some think that maybe baptism should come first.

No, Jesus says "believe"

A gospel chorus says, "Only believe".   I have never liked that song because the emphasis always seems to be on the word "only" rather than "believe". But it is true. Believe. Nothing less. Nothing more.

You may feel like the father who brought his son to Jesus for healing:
"Jesus said to him, 'If you can believe, all things are possible to him who believes.' Immediately the father of the child cried out with tears, "I believe. Help my unbelief!'"
Mark 9:33,34

Lord, I believe.

CHALLENGE: TO LET THE WORK OF GOD BE DONE IN ME AS I BELIEVE IN THE ONE HE SENT.

Prayer:

LORD, I want to open my life in faith to become the disciple you called me to be. Amen.

DAILY DEVOTIONAL 22

Scripture Reading: John 6:35-59

JESUS IS THE BREAD OF LIFE

6:35. Jesus said to them, "I am the bread of life. Whoever comes to me will not be hungry, and whoever believes in me will never be thirsty. 36. But I told you that you have seen me, and yet you don't believe.37. All those whom the Father gives me will come to me. He who comes to me I will in no way throw out.
38. For I have come down from heaven, not to do my own will, but the will of him who sent me.

39. This is the will of my Father who sent me, that of all he has given to me I should lose nothing, but should raise him up at the last day.
40. This is the will of the one who sent me, that everyone who sees the Son, and believes in him, should have eternal life; and I will raise him up at the last day."
41. The Jews therefore murmured concerning him, because he said, "I am the bread which came down out of heaven." ...

48. I am the bread of life.
49. Your fathers ate the manna in the wilderness, and they died.
50. This is the bread which comes down out of heaven, that anyone may eat of it and not die.
51. I am the living bread which came down out of heaven. If anyone eats of this bread, he will live forever. Yes, the bread which I will give for the life of the world is my flesh."...
55. For my flesh is food indeed, and my blood is drink indeed.
56. He who eats my flesh and drinks my blood lives in me, and I in him.
57. As the living Father sent me, and I live because of the Father; so he who feeds on me, he will also live because of Me. ...

* * * * * * * * * * * * * * *

JIM'S THOUGHT FOR THE DAY

"I am the bread of life." vs. 35

This is the first of seven "I am ..." saying of Jesus in the Gospel of John. We have already noted the seven "signs". We will take note of each of the seven "I am ..." sayings as we continue through the Gospel.

I AM:

...The bread of life 6:36   ...The light of the world 8:12

...The sheep's door 10:7   ...The good shepherd 10:11

...The resurrection and the life 11:25

...The way, the truth and the life 14:6

...The true vine 15:1

Bread was thought of as the substance of life. God is seen as the divine provider. Jesus reminds them of when God provided the manna in the wilderness for the children of Israel. Enough manna was provided for each day. God's provision was sufficient. (Exodus 16)

The language about eating his body and drinking his blood was not meant to be taken literally but spiritually. Many people in Jesus' day offered sacrifices to pagan gods. When they ate the meat from these sacrifices they thought they were partaking of the god into their bodies. Jesus would use this symbolism in the Last Supper. We spiritually partake of him when we partake of the bread and cup.

CHALLENGE: TO RECOGNIZE JESUS AS THE SUSTAINER OF MY SPIRITUAL LIFE AND TO PARTAKE OF HIM.

Prayer:

LORD, Thank you for every good and perfect gift. Your presence within me brings fulfillment and joy. Amen.

DAILY DEVOTIONAL 23

Scripture Reading: John 6:60-71 (WEB)

THE HARD SAYINGS OF JESUS

60 Therefore many of his disciples, when they heard this, said, "This is a hard saying! Who can listen to it?"

61 But Jesus knowing in himself that his disciples murmured at this, said to them, "Does this cause you to stumble? 62 Then what if you would see the Son of Man ascending to where he was before? 63 It is the spirit who gives life. The flesh profits nothing. The words that I speak to you are spirit, and are life. 64 But there are some of you who don't believe."

For Jesus knew from the beginning who they were who didn't believe, and who it was who would betray him. 65 He said, "For this cause I have said to you that no one can come to me, unless it is given to him by my Father."

66 At this, many of his disciples went back, and walked no more with him. 67 Jesus said therefore to the twelve, "You don't also want to go away, do you?"

68 Simon Peter answered him, "Lord, to whom would we go? You have the words of eternal life. 69 We have come to believe and know that you are the Christ, the Son of the living God."

70 Jesus answered them, "Didn't I choose you, the twelve, and one of you is a devil?" 71 Now he spoke of Judas, the son of Simon Iscariot, for it was he who would betray him, being one of the twelve.

* * * * * * * * * * * * * * * *

JIM'S THOUGHT FOR THE DAY

What is your "hard saying".

"Therefore many of his disciples, when they heard this, said, "This is a hard saying!" vs. 60 A number of years ago I read a book with the title "The Hard Sayings of Jesus". The author listed 70 sayings of Jesus that are challenging and difficult to follow.

What is the hardest saying of Jesus that comes to your mind?
Turn the other cheek.
Love your enemies.
Be perfect.
Take up your cross.
Have faith that moves mountains.
Sell what you have.

The "hard saying" of Jesus to those hearing Jesus was to accept that he was from God, the bread of life.

This "hard saying" challenges me:
"For if you forgive men their trespasses, your heavenly Father will also forgive you. But if you don't forgive men their trespasses, neither will your Father forgive your trespasses." Matthew 6:14, 15. I confess to finding this challenging. The hard sayings of Jesus are to challenge and help us, not to discourage and condemn us.

Pay attention to what he says!

CHALLENGE: TO RESPOND TO THE WORDS OF JESUS IN A PERSONAL WAY, ACCEPTING THAT HIS WAY IS THE BRST WAY FOR MY LIFE.

Prayer:

LORD, Forgive me when I neglect to take seriously your commands in my life. Give me the courage of obedience. Amen.

DAILY DEVOTIONAL 24

Scripture Reading: John 7:1-13 (WEB)

YOUR TIME IS ALWAYS READY

7:1 After these things, Jesus was walking in Galilee, for he wouldn't walk in Judea, because the Jews sought to kill him. 2 Now the feast of the Jews, the Feast of Booths, was at hand. 3 His brothers therefore said to him, "Depart from here and go into Judea, that your disciples also may see your works which you do. 4 For no one does anything in secret while he seeks to be known openly. If you do these things, reveal yourself to the world." 5 For even his brothers didn't believe in him.

6 Jesus therefore said to them, "My time has not yet come, but your time is always ready. 7 The world can't hate you, but it hates me, because I testify about it, that its works are evil. 8 You go up to the feast. I am not yet going up to this feast, because my time is not yet fulfilled."

9 Having said these things to them, he stayed in Galilee. 10 But when his brothers had gone up to the feast, then he also went up, not publicly, but as it were in secret. 11 The Jews therefore sought him at the feast, and said, "Where is he?"

12 There was much murmuring among the multitudes concerning him. Some said, "He is a good man." Others said, "Not so, but he leads the multitude astray." 13 Yet no one spoke openly of him for fear of the Jews.

* * * * * * * * * * * * * * *

JIM'S THOUGHT FOR THE DAY

"Jesus therefore said to them, 'My time has not yet come, but your time is always ready.'" vs. 6

Did you ever say, "I'll do it when the time is right?" Sometimes this is said seriously but most often it is said to delay an action we do not want to take. It is a good way to make an excuse.

Is there something in your life that needs to be done that you have kept putting off until "the right time"? Maybe it is to reconcile a relationship. Maybe to forgive someone. Maybe to stop a bad habit. Maybe to do a kind deed. Maybe to ask for forgiveness.

Beware of putting off what you need to do.

The word for time that Jesus uses in this passage relates to the time of opportunity not the time on the calendar. Jesus is saying that this is your time of opportunity to follow me, to serve me, to obey me. And opportunities often close. Squandered opportunities may be lost forever.

Now is your time!

CHALLENGE: TO USE MY TIME OF OPPORTUNITY TO ACT ON GOD'S WILL AND PURPOSE AND TO NOT FAIL HIM.

Prayer:

LORD, give me the courage to act during my times of opportunity. Help me not to delay in doing your will. Amen

DAILY DEVOTIONAL 25

Scripture Reading: John 7:14-24

DESIRE TO DO HIS WILL

14 But when it was now the middle of the feast, Jesus went up into the temple and taught. 15 The Jews therefore marveled, saying, "How does this man know letters, having never been educated?"

16 Jesus therefore answered them, "My teaching is not mine, but his who sent me. 17 If anyone desires to do his will, he will know about the teaching, whether it is from God, or if I am speaking from myself.

18 He who speaks from himself seeks his own glory, but he who seeks the glory of him who sent him is true, and no unrighteousness is in him. 19 Didn't Moses give you the law, and yet none of you keeps the law? Why do you seek to kill me?"

20 The multitude answered, "You have a demon! Who seeks to kill you?"

21 Jesus answered them, "I did one work and you all marvel because of it. 22 Moses has given you circumcision (not that it is of Moses, but of the fathers), and on the Sabbath you circumcise a boy. 23 If a boy receives circumcision on the Sabbath, that the law of Moses may not be broken, are you angry with me, because I made a man completely healthy on the Sabbath? 24 Don't judge according to appearance, but judge righteous judgment."

* * * * * * * * * * * * * * *

JIM'S THOUGHT FOR THE DAY

"If anyone desires to do his will, he will know about the teaching, whether it is from God, or if I am speaking from myself." vs. 17

What is your heart's desire? What really matters to you? What do you long for?

David once said, "As the deer pants for the water brooks, so my soul pants after you, God. My soul thirsts for God, for the living God." Psalm 42:1

Such spiritual desire leads to a joyful relationship with God. The illustrations of satisfying spiritual thirst and hunger come into focus. God satisfies the longing within us. No one else can.

Do you really desire to know and follow his will?

CHALLENGE: TO DEVELOP A DESIRE FOR GOD THAT GROWN AND FINDS FULFILLMENT IN MY WORSHIPPING AND SERVING HIM.

Prayer:

LORD, I thank you for hungering and thirsting for righteousness. Satisfy my soul with your presence. Amen.

DAILY DEVOTIONAL 26

Scripture Reading: John 7:25-34 (WEB)

THE ONE GOD SENT

6:25 Therefore some of them of Jerusalem said, "Isn't this he whom they seek to kill? 26 Behold, he speaks openly, and they say nothing to him. Can it be that the rulers indeed know that this is truly the Christ? 27 However we know where this man comes from, but when the Christ comes, no one will know where he comes from."

28 Jesus therefore cried out in the temple, teaching and saying, "You both know me, and know where I am from. I have not come of myself, but he who sent me is true, whom you don't know. 29 I know him, because I am from him, and he sent me."

30 They sought therefore to take him; but no one laid a hand on him, because his hour had not yet come. 31 But of the multitude, many believed in him. They said, "When the Christ comes, he won't do more signs than those which this man has done, will he?"

32 The Pharisees heard the multitude murmuring these things concerning him, and the chief priests and the Pharisees sent officers to arrest him.

33 Then Jesus said, "I will be with you a little while longer, then I go to him who sent me. 34 You will seek me, and won't find me. You can't come where I am."

* * * * * * * * * * * * *

JIM'S THOUGHT FOR THE DAY

"I have not come of myself, but he who sent me is true" vs. 28

John continues to make the all important point that Jesus was sent by the Father to provide for our eternal life. In John 10:10 Jesus said "I came that they may have life, and may have it abundantly."

Have you ever ask, "Who said so?" Who says or does something is all important. Jesus verified his authority as coming from God the Father himself. He claims that authority. What he says is eternally true. He said, "I know him, because I am from him, and he sent me." vs. 29

Those who follow Jesus recognize and acknowledge that his words have authority and power.

His word is the last word!

CHALLENGE: TO LISTEN TO THE WORDS OF JESUS AND HE HAS THE WORDS OF ETERNAL LIFE.

Prayer:

LORD, Give me spiritual ears to hear, acknowledge and obey your works of truth. Amen

DAILY DEVOTIONAL 27

Scripture Reading: John 7: 37-52 (WEB)

THE FAITH JOURNEY OF NICODEMUS

37 Now on the last and greatest day of the feast, Jesus stood and cried out, "If anyone is thirsty, let him come to me and drink! 38 He who believes in me, as the Scripture has said, from within him will flow rivers of living water." 39 But he said this about the Spirit, which those believing in him were to receive. For the Holy Spirit was not yet given, because Jesus wasn't yet glorified.

40 Many of the multitude therefore, when they heard these words, said, "This is truly the prophet." 41 Others said, "This is the Christ." But some said, "What, does the Christ come out of Galilee? 42 Hasn't the Scripture said that the Christ comes of the offspring[a] of David, and from Bethlehem, the village where David was?" 43 So a division arose in the multitude because of him. 44 Some of them would have arrested him, but no one laid hands on him. 45 The officers therefore came to the chief priests and Pharisees, and they said to them, "Why didn't you bring him?"
46 The officers answered, "No man ever spoke like this man!"

47 The Pharisees therefore answered them, "You aren't also led astray, are you? 48 Have any of the rulers believed in him, or of the Pharisees? 49 But this multitude that doesn't know the law is cursed."
50 Nicodemus (he who came to him by night, being one of them) said to them, 51 "Does our law judge a man, unless it first hears from him personally and knows what he does?

52 They answered him, "Are you also from Galilee? Search, and see that no prophet has arisen out of Galilee."

* * * * * * * * * * * * * * *

JIM'S THOUGHT FOR THE DAY

Nicodemus is mentioned three times in the Gospel of John. (And not mentioned any other place in the Bible.) In John 3 we are told that he came to Jesus one night as a seeker. His conversation with Jesus climaxed with the verse, "For God so loved the world..." John 3:16. We are not told in that passage what response Nicodemus made to Jesus.

Here in John 7 Nicodemus comes to the defense of Jesus when he is condemned by the Pharisees. Still we are not told what response he has made to Jesus.

In John 20 we are told that Nicodemus brought spices to anoint the body of the crucified Jesus. It is obvious now that he and Joseph of Arimathaea had become believing followers of Jesus as they buried the body of Jesus.

Sometimes faith come to a person quickly. To others it is a long journey of months or years. Our spiritual journeys are not all alike. But in one way they are all alike- they are all personal.

Nicodemus completed the journey of faith. I would like to know more about his journey and what he did after the resurrection but I must wait for heaven to find that out.

It is enough to know that he completed the journey of faith. I hope and pray that you have too.

CHALLENGE: TO BE AN OPEN DISCIPLE OF JESUS WITHOUT RESERVATION.

Prayer:

LORD, I want to be a bold witness of my faith. Help me to tell the world that I'm a Christian. Amen.

DAILY DEVOTIONAL 28

Scripture Reading: John 7:53-8:11

CASTING THE FIRST STONE

7:53 Everyone went to his own house, 8:1 but Jesus went to the Mount of Olives. 2 Now very early in the morning, he came again into the temple, and all the people came to him. He sat down and taught them.

3 The scribes and the Pharisees brought a woman taken in adultery. Having set her in the middle, 4 they told him, "Teacher, we found this woman in adultery, in the very act. 5 Now in our law, Moses commanded us to stone such women. What then do you say about her?" 6 They said this testing him, that they might have something to accuse him of.

But Jesus stooped down and wrote on the ground with his finger.

7 But when they continued asking him, he looked up and said to them, "He who is without sin among you, let him throw the first stone at her." 8 Again he stooped down and wrote on the ground with his finger.

9 They, when they heard it, being convicted by their conscience, went out one by one, beginning from the oldest, even to the last. Jesus was left alone with the woman where she was, in the middle. 10 Jesus, standing up, saw her and said, "Woman, where are your accusers? Did no one condemn you?"
11 She said, "No one, Lord."
Jesus said, "Neither do I condemn you. Go your way. From now on, sin no more."

* * * * * * * * * * * * *

JIM'S THOUGHT FOR THE DAY

You may find a foot note in your Bible that this passage in not in some of the oldest Biblical manuscripts. The reason most often assumed is that some early Scribes did not feel comfortable with a story about such a sinful woman and simply omitted the story when they copied the text.

There is no reason to think that the passage does not record an actual event in the life of Jesus.

Jesus was accused of associating with sinners. Here he acts with compassion toward a woman degraded by religious leaders.

And do not miss his challenge, "He who is without sin among you, let him throw the first stone at her." vs. 7.

But my curiosity keeps asking "What did Jesus write on the ground?" What he said and what he wrote caused the woman's accusers to go away without further accusations.

He might have written "Love". He might have written about their sins. We do not know, but the lesson is clear. You and I are not qualified to judge. Compassion and forgiveness are the characteristics of Jesus followers.

And don't neglect to remember Jesus' words: "From now on, sin no more".

CHALLENGE: TO NOT CONDEMN THOSE WHO SIN BUT TRY TO LOVE THEM AND RESTORE THEM TO GOODNESS.

Prayer:

LORD, Give me a compassion heart for those in need of your forgiveness. Amen.

DAILY DEVOTIONAL 29

Scripture Reading: John 8:12-20

I AM THE LIGHT OF THE WORLD

12 Again, therefore, Jesus spoke to them, saying, "I am the light of the world. He who follows me will not walk in the darkness, but will have the light of life."

13 The Pharisees therefore said to him, "You testify about yourself. Your testimony is not valid."

14 Jesus answered them, "Even if I testify about myself, my testimony is true, for I know where I came from, and where I am going; but you don't know where I came from, or where I am going. 15 You judge according to the flesh. I judge no one. 16 Even if I do judge, my judgment is true, for I am not alone, but I am with the Father who sent me. 17 It's also written in your law that the testimony of two people is valid. 18. I am one who testifies about myself, and the Father who sent me testifies about me."

19 They said therefore to him, "Where is your Father?"
Jesus answered, "You know neither me nor my Father. If you knew me, you would know my Father also."

20 Jesus spoke these words in the treasury, as he taught in the temple. Yet no one arrested him, because his hour had not yet come.

* * * * * * * * * * *

JIM'S THOUGHT FOR THE DAY

"He who follows me will not walk in the darkness, but will have the light of life." vs. 12

This passage gives us the second "I am..." saying of Jesus: "I am the light of the world". The result is that we have the light of life. Therefore, we do not walk in darkness.

Being brought up in the city, I was always use to light: electric lamps, flash lights, street lights, etc. One summer during my Seminary years I lived in a rural Kentucky community. There were no street lights and limited electric lights. For the first time I experienced darkness.

Darkness is frightful. Darkness is disorienting. Darkness is dangerous. Darkness keeps us from seeing.

These results of physical darkness are multiplied by spiritual darkness. Without spiritual light we are lost, confused, afraid and blind.

The familiar gospel song says: "Once I was blind, but now I see."

"The light of the world is Jesus."

Jesus said we are to be lights. "Let your light shine before men, that they may see your good works and glorify your Father who is in heaven." Matthew 5:16

CHALLENGE: TO FOLLOW THE LIGHT GOD HAS GIVEN ME AND TO BE A LIGHT IN A DARK WORLD.

Prayer:

LORD, No more darkness, no more night. I will walk with you. Amen.

DAILY DEVOTIONAL 30

Scripture Reading: John 8:21-30

ALWAYS DO THE THINGS THAT ARE PLEASING TO HIM

21 Jesus said therefore again to them, "I am going away, and you will seek me, and you will die in your sins. Where I go, you can't come."

22 The Jews therefore said, "Will he kill himself, because he says, 'Where I am going, you can't come'?"

23 He said to them, "You are from beneath. I am from above. You are of this world. I am not of this world. 24 I said therefore to you that you will die in your sins; for unless you believe that I am he, you will die in your sins."

25 They said therefore to him, "Who are you?"

Jesus said to them, "Just what I have been saying to you from the beginning. 26 I have many things to speak and to judge concerning you. However he who sent me is true; and the things which I heard from him, these I say to the world."

27 They didn't understand that he spoke to them about the Father. 28 Jesus therefore said to them, "When you have lifted up the Son of Man, then you will know that I am he, and I do nothing of myself, but as my Father taught me, I say these things. 29 He who sent me is with me. The Father hasn't left me alone, for I always do the things that are pleasing to him."

30 As he spoke these things, many believed in him.

* * * * * * * * * * * *

JIM'S THOUGHT FOR THE DAY

"I always do the things that are pleasing to him." vs. 29

When you truly love someone you desire to please them. And great joy comes in doing so.

It was the intent and desire of Jesus to please his Father in heaven. At his baptism it is recorded that a voice out of the sky said: "You are my beloved Son in whom I am well pleased." Mark 1:11

Is it your ultimate desire to please God? How can you please him?

You please God by your praise.
You please God by your worship.
You please God by your faith.
You please God by your obedience.
You please God by your service.
You please God by your fellowship.
You please God by talking with him.
You please God by telling others about him.
You please God by honoring him.
You please God by loving him.

CHALLENGE: TO PLEASE GOD IN EVERY AREA OF MY LIFE.

Prayer:

LORD, I pray that I will honor you in the way I live and in the way I treat others. Amen.

DAILY DEVOTIONAL 31

Scripture Reading: John 8:31-41 (WEB)

FREE INDEED!

31 Jesus therefore said to those Jews who had believed him, "If you remain in my word, then you are truly my disciples. 32 You will know the truth, and the truth will make you free."

33 They answered him, "We are Abraham's offspring, and have never been in bondage to anyone. How do you say, 'You will be made free'?"

34 Jesus answered them, "Most certainly I tell you, everyone who commits sin is the bondservant of sin. 35 A bondservant doesn't live in the house forever. A son remains forever. 36 If therefore the Son makes you free, you will be free indeed.

37 I know that you are Abraham's offspring, yet you seek to kill me, because my word finds no place in you. 38 I say the things which I have seen with my Father; and you also do the things which you have seen with your father."

39 They answered him, "Our father is Abraham."

Jesus said to them, "If you were Abraham's children, you would do the works of Abraham. 40 But now you seek to kill me, a man who has told you the truth which I heard from God. Abraham didn't do this. 41 You do the works of your father."

* * * * * * * * * * * *

JIM'S THOUGHT FOR THE DAY

"If therefore the Son makes you free, you will be free indeed." vs. 36

Jesus says everyone who commits sin is the "bondservant of sin". vs. 34. A bondservant was the lowest level of servitude. A bondservant had no rights. He had no hope of redemption or freedom. He was looked upon as a "thing", not a person. He was a possession. He had no choices of his own.

We are helpless in our sin. We are bondservant. We cannot change our relationship by ourselves.

But we are not without hope! Jesus is the "chain breaker".

"If you've got pain, He's a pain taker.
If you feel lost, He's a way maker.
If you need freedom or saving, He's a prison-shaking Savior.
If you've got chains, He's a chain breaker!"

We are transformed by faith in Jesus from a bondservant to a son. And "a son remains forever". vs. 35

The slave song says: "Free at last. Free at last. Praise God Almighty. I'm free at last".

CHALLENGE: TO ENJOY THE POSITION OF A SON OF GOD FREE FROM THE BONDAGES OF SIN AND FREE TO CLAIM THE RIGHTS OF A CHILD OF GOD.

Prayer:

LORD, Thank you for my freedom in Christ. Thank you for setting me free from the bondage of sin and death. Amen.

DAILY DEVOTIONAL 32

Scripture Reading: John 8:48-59

HE IS THE "I AM"

8:48 Then the Jews answered him, "Don't we say well that you are a Samaritan, and have a demon?"

49 Jesus answered, "I don't have a demon, but I honor my Father and you dishonor me. 50 But I don't seek my own glory. There is one who seeks and judges. 51 Most certainly, I tell you, if a person keeps my word, he will never see death."

52 Then the Jews said to him, "Now we know that you have a demon. Abraham died, as did the prophets; and you say, 'If a man keeps my word, he will never taste of death.' 53 Are you greater than our father, Abraham, who died? The prophets died. Who do you make yourself out to be?"

54 Jesus answered, "If I glorify myself, my glory is nothing. It is my Father who glorifies me, of whom you say that he is our God. 55 You have not known him, but I know him. If I said, 'I don't know him,' I would be like you, a liar. But I know him and keep his word. 56 Your father Abraham rejoiced to see my day. He saw it, and was glad."
57 The Jews therefore said to him, "You are not yet fifty years old! Have you seen Abraham?"

58 Jesus said to them, "Most certainly, I tell you, before Abraham came into existence, I AM."

59 Therefore they took up stones to throw at him, but Jesus was hidden, and went out of the temple, having gone through the middle of them, and so passed by.

* * * * * * * * * * * *

66

JIM'S THOUGHT FOR THE DAY

"Jesus said to them, "Most certainly, I tell you, before Abraham came into existence, I AM." vs. 58 Jesus is the great "I Am"!

The personal name for God comes from "to be". He is the eternal one, the one who has always been.

Thus Jesus could say, "Before Moses came into existence, I AM."

The first verse in the gospel tells us: "In the beginning was the Word, and the Word was with God, and the Word was God. The same was in the beginning with God. All things were made through him. Without him, nothing was made that has been made." John 1:1-3.

Over and over Jesus has proclaimed that he and the Father are one. His ability to forgive our sins is based on this fact. Jesus was not just a good man, a master teacher or a prophet. He was and is eternal God. Thus he could be the sacrifice for our sins.

You and I need to acknowledge him as "my Lord and my God". He is worthy to be praised.

CHALLENGE: TO GLORIFY JESUS AS ETERNAL GOD WHO LOVES US, CARES FOR US AND FORGIVES US.

Prayer:

LORD, I thank you that because I believe I will never see death. Amen.

DAILY DEVOTIONAL 33

Scripture Reading: John 9:1-41 (WEB)

LORD, I BELIEVE

9:1 As he passed by, he saw a man blind from birth. 2 His disciples asked him, "Rabbi, who sinned, this man or his parents, that he was born blind?"

3 Jesus answered, "This man didn't sin, nor did his parents; but, that the works of God might be revealed in him. 4 I must work the works of him who sent me while it is day. The night is coming, when no one can work. 5 While I am in the world, I am the light of the world." 6 When he had said this, he spat on the ground, made mud with the saliva, anointed the blind man's eyes with the mud, 7 and said to him, "Go, wash in the pool of Siloam" (which means "Sent"). So he went away, washed, and came back seeing. 8 The neighbors therefore, and those who saw that he was blind before, said, "Isn't this he who sat and begged?" 9 Others were saying, "It is he." Still others were saying, "He looks like him."

He said, "I am he."

He said, "He is a prophet." ...

35 Jesus heard that they had thrown him out, and finding him, he said, "Do you believe in the Son of God?"

36 He answered, "Who is he, Lord, that I may believe in him?"

37 Jesus said to him, "You have both seen him, and it is he who speaks with you."

38 He said, "Lord, I believe!" and he worshiped him.

39 Jesus said, "I came into this world for judgment, that those who don't see may see; and that those who see may become blind."

40 Those of the Pharisees who were with him heard these things, and said to him, "Are we also blind?"

41 Jesus said to them, "If you were blind, you would have no sin; but now you say, 'We see.' Therefore your sin remains.

* * * * * * * * * * * * * * * * * *

JIM'S THOUGHT FOR THE DAY

"He said, 'Lord, I believe!' and he worshiped him." vs. 38

This amazing story takes up the entire 9th chapter of John's gospel. Our daily scripture reading has been about 12 verses long, but today the entire chapter is included to keep the story intact. Please read the entire chapter in your Bible.

This is the sixth "sign" in the gospel of John. As such it is about more than a physical miracle. The sign teaches us about receiving spiritual sight. It affirms again the deity of Jesus. He is the Son of God.

Notice the progress of this man's response to Jesus.
He begins by calling Jesus a man. vs. 11
He goes on to call Jesus a prophet. vs. 17
Finally, he came to confess that Jesus was Lord, the Son of God. vss. 35, 38. And he worshipped him.

The Pharisees could not see the sign Jesus gave them. They were more concerned about keeping the Sabbath rules than the healing of a blind man. They were spiritually blind. They said, "We see" but they did not see.

Do you see the signs God gives? Open your spiritual eyes. Say it: "Lord, I believe".

CHALLENGE: TO SEE WHAT GOD IS DOING ALL AROUND ME AND TO KEEP MY SPIRIYUAL EYES OPEN AND FOCUSED ON HIM.

Prayer:

LORD, Open my eyes that I might see glimpses of truth you have for me. Open my eyes, illuminate me. Amen.

DAILY DEVOTIONAL 34

Scripture Reading: John 10:1-10 (WEB)

I AM THE DOOR

10.1 Most certainly, I tell you, one who doesn't enter by the door into the sheep fold, but climbs up some other way, the same is a thief and a robber.

2But one who enters in by the door is the shepherd of the sheep. 3The gatekeeper opens the gate for him, and the sheep listen to his voice. He calls his own sheep by name, and leads them out.

4Whenever he brings out his own sheep, he goes before them, and the sheep follow him, for they know his voice. 5They will by no means follow a stranger, but will flee from him; for they don't know the voice of strangers."

6Jesus spoke this parable to them, but they didn't understand what he was telling them.⁰ᴮᴶ

7Jesus therefore said to them again, "Most certainly, I tell you, I am the sheep's door. 8All who came before me are thieves and robbers, but the sheep didn't listen to them.

9I am the door. If anyone enters in by me, he will be saved, and will go in and go out, and will find pasture. 10The thief only comes to steal, kill, and destroy. I came that they may have life, and may have it abundantly.

* * * * * * * * * * * * *

JIM'S THOUGHT FOR THE DAY

Here we have the third "I am..." saying of Jesus: "I am the sheep's door". vs. 7

Jesus gives a parable about a shepherd and his sheep. Those who first heard it were familiar with the life of a shepherd. Most sheep were raised for their wool. Therefore a shepherd would often have a sheep for many years. A special relationship developed. The sheep knew the voice of the shepherd. The sheep learned to follow the shepherd. The shepherd called his sheep by name.

When the shepherd kept his sheep out in the field at night, he often put them in a stone made pen. The pen usually had no door. The shepherd would lay down in the opening to the pen. He became the "door".

The purpose of Jesus is specific. "I am the door. If anyone enters in by me, he will be saved ... I came that they may have life, and may have it abundantly." vs. 9,10

"Jesus spoke this parable to them, but they didn't understand what he was telling them." vs. 6

Jesus said that his sheep hear his voice. The illustration of light and seeing is followed by that of hearing.

Do you listen for his voice?

CHALLENGE: TO LISTEN FOR THE VOICE OF THE SHEPHERD AND TO FOLLOW.

Prayer:

LORD, Thank you for being the protective door in my life and for being the way to the abundant life. Amen.

DAILY DEVOTIONAL 35

Scripture Reading: John 10:11-18 (WEB)

THE GOOD SHEPHERD

10:11 I am the good shepherd. The good shepherd lays down his life for the sheep.

12 He who is a hired hand, and not a shepherd, who doesn't own the sheep, sees the wolf coming, leaves the sheep, and flees. The wolf snatches the sheep, and scatters them.

13 The hired hand flees because he is a hired hand, and doesn't care for the sheep.

14 I am the good shepherd. I know my own, and I'm known by my own; 15 even as the Father knows me, and I know the Father. I lay down my life for the sheep.

16 I have other sheep, which are not of this fold. I must bring them also, and they will hear my voice. They will become one flock with one shepherd.

17 Therefore the Father loves me, because I lay down my life, that I may take it again. 18 No one takes it away from me, but I lay it down by myself. I have power to lay it down, and I have power to take it again. I received this commandment from my Father."

* * * * * * * * * * * *

JIM'S THOUGHT FOR THE DAY

" I am the good shepherd" is the fourth of the "I am..." sayings.

Twice in this passage Jesus says that he lays down his life for the sheep. Not only is he the good shepherd, he is the Lamb of God who takes away the sin of the world. He said, "I lay down my life". vs. 17

When I read the 23rd Psalm, I always add these words of Jesus. "I am the good shepherd."

Jesus knows your name!

A little girl had memorized the 23rd Psalm and very proudly she was quoting it to her grandparents. She started it this way: "The Lord is my shepherd, what else could I want?"

She may have missed the familiar words, but she did not miss the meaning of the psalm.

If the Lord is your shepherd, what else could you want?

CHALLENGE: TO LISTEN TO THE VOICE OF THE GOOD SHEPHERD AND TO FOLLOW HIM.

Prayer:

LORD, Thank you for being my shepherd and my savior. I commit myself to follow you. Amen.

DAILY DEVOTIONAL 36

Scripture Read: John 10:19-30 (WEB)

NO ONE IS ABLE TO SNATCH THEM OUT OF MY FATHER'S HAND

10:19 Therefore a division arose again among the Jews because of these words. 20 Many of them said, "He has a demon, and is insane! Why do you listen to him?" 21 Others said, "These are not the sayings of one possessed by a demon. It isn't possible for a demon to open the eyes of the blind, is it?"

22 It was the Feast of the Dedication at Jerusalem. 23 It was winter, and Jesus was walking in the temple, in Solomon's porch. 24 The Jews therefore came around him and said to him, "How long will you hold us in suspense? If you are the Christ, tell us plainly."

25 Jesus answered them, "I told you, and you don't believe. The works that I do in my Father's name, these testify about me. 26 But you don't believe, because you are not of my sheep, as I told you.

27 My sheep hear my voice, and I know them, and they follow me.

28 I give eternal life to them. They will never perish, and no one will snatch them out of my hand.

29 My Father who has given them to me is greater than all. No one is able to snatch them out of my Father's hand. 30 I and the Father are one."

* * * * * * * * * * * * *

JIM'S THOUGHT FOR THE DAY

This passage talks about the security of the believer. Baptists often use the term "Once saved, always saved", but that is not a biblical phrase. Some interpret that phrase to mean a person who claims to be saved can live like the devil and not lose his salvation. That is not biblical either.

What is biblical is the truth stated here. The Lord who saves us keeps us. Once we put ourselves in the hands of Jesus we are eternally secure.

"My Father who has given them to me is greater than all. No one is able to snatch them out of my Father's hand". vs. 29

"Blessed assurance, Jesus is mine!"

Eternal life is just that - eternal. A Sunday school teacher ask his class of young boys, "What is eternal?" One answered, "Eternal is somethin' that don't ever quit".

In Christ we have eternal life that never quits. "When we've been there ten thousand years ... We've no less days to sing God's praise than when we first begun."

CHALLENGE: TO. CLAIN THE PROMISE OF GOD FOR SALVATION THAT IS ETERNAL BECAUSE OF HIS POWER AND GRACE.

Prayer:

LORD, Give me the joy of thy salvation knowing that I am secure in your hands. Amen.

DAILY DEVOTIONAL 37

Scripture Reading: John 10:31-42 (WEB)

EVERYTHING JOHN SAID ABOUT THIS MAN IS TRUE

10:31 Therefore Jews took up stones again to stone him. 32Jesus answered them, "I have shown you many good works from my Father. For which of those works do you stone me?"

33The Jews answered him, "We don't stone you for a good work, but for blasphemy: because you, being a man, make yourself God."

34Jesus answered them, "Isn't it written in your law, 'I said, you are gods?' 35If he called them gods, to whom the word of God came (and the Scripture can't be broken), 36do you say of him whom the Father sanctified and sent into the world, 'You blaspheme,' because I said, 'I am the Son of God?'

37If I don't do the works of my Father, don't believe me. 38But if I do them, though you don't believe me, believe the works; that you may know and believe that the Father is in me, and I in the Father."

39They sought again to seize him, and he went out of their hand.

40He went away again beyond the Jordan into the place where John was baptizing at first, and there he stayed. 41Many came to him.

They said, "John indeed did no sign, but everything that John said about this man is true." 42Many believed in him there.

* * * * * * * * * * * * *

JIM'S THOUGHT FOR THE DAY

"Everything that John said about this man is true." vs. 41

What had John said about Jesus?

John said:

"Behold the Lamb of God
Who takes away the sin of the world."

"He must increase and I must decrease."

"This is he of whom I said, 'After me comes a man who is preferred before me, for he was before me.'"

"I didn't know him, but for this reason I came baptizing in water: that he would be revealed to Israel."

"I have seen the Spirit descending like a dove out of heaven, and it remained on him. I didn't recognize him, but he who sent me to baptize in water said to me, 'On whomever you will see the Spirit descending and remaining on him is he who baptizes in the Holy Spirit.'

"I have seen, and have testified that this is the Son of God."

Jesus is the fulfillment of Old Testament prophesy. John was sent by God to prepare the way for him.

CHALLENGE: TO ACKNOWLEDGE JESUS AS THE LAMB OF GOD: THE SUPREME SACRIFICE FOR OUR SINS.

Prayer:

LORD, I accept your gift of salvation with joy and gratitude.
Amen.

DAILY DEVOTIONAL 38

Scripture Reading: John 11:1-10

BUT FOR THE GLORY OF GOD

11:1 Now a certain man was sick, Lazarus from Bethany, of the village of Mary and her sister, Martha. 2It was that Mary who had anointed the Lord with ointment, and wiped his feet with her hair, whose brother, Lazarus, was sick.

3The sisters therefore sent to him, saying, "Lord, behold, he for whom you have great affection is sick." 4But when Jesus heard it, he said, "This sickness is not to death, but for the glory of God, that God's Son may be glorified by it."

5Now Jesus loved Martha, and her sister, and Lazarus. 6When therefore he heard that he was sick, he stayed two days in the place where he was.

7Then after this he said to the disciples, "Let's go into Judea again."

8The disciples told him, "Rabbi, the Jews were just trying to stone you, and are you going there again?"

9Jesus answered, "Aren't there twelve hours of daylight? If a man walks in the day, he doesn't stumble, because he sees the light of this world.

10But if a man walks in the night, he stumbles, because the light isn't in him."

* * * * * * * * * * * * *

JIM'S THOUGHT FOR THE DAY

"This sickness is not to death, but for the glory of God, that God's Son may be glorified by it." vs. 4

This entire chapter is about the resurrection of Lazarus and the response to it.

Many things that happen to us are difficult to understand. We struggle to understand when God does not answer our prayers immediately. We question how God can use difficult circumstances in our lives. We want to believe that God works in all things for good.

The disciples and Mary and Martha did not understand why Jesus delayed going to Bethany when he was informed that Lazarus was sick. But there was divine purpose in what Jesus did.

God has a perfect plan for our lives. We need to understand that his ways are not the same as our ways. We cannot see the future but he can.

Jesus assured his disciples that what was happening in the life and death of Lazarus was "for the glory of God, that God's Son may be glorified by it." vs. 4

When they knew "the rest of the story" they would understand. And you and I "will understand it better by and by."

CHALLENGE: TO UNDERSTAND THAT NOW WE ONLY SEE THROUGH A "GLASS, DARKLY". OUR UNDERSTANDING OF GOD'S PLAN IS LIMITED BUT HIS PLAN IS PERFECT.

Prayer:

LORD, Give me patience to wait upon you. I want you to be glorified. Amen.

DAILY DEVOTIONAL 39

Scripture Reading: John 11:12-21

LORD, IF YOU WOULD HAVE BEEN HERE

12:11He said these things, and after that, he said to them, "Our friend, Lazarus, has fallen asleep, but I am going so that I may awake him out of sleep."

12 The disciples therefore said, "Lord, if he has fallen asleep, he will recover."

13 Now Jesus had spoken of his death, but they thought that he spoke of taking rest in sleep. 14 So Jesus said to them plainly then, "Lazarus is dead. 15 I am glad for your sakes that I was not there, so that you may believe. Nevertheless, let's go to him."

16 Thomas therefore, who is called Didymus, said to his fellow disciples, "Let's go also, that we may die with him."

17 So when Jesus came, he found that he had been in the tomb four days already. 18 Now Bethany was near Jerusalem, about fifteen stadia away.

19 Many of the Jews had joined the women around Martha and Mary, to console them concerning their brother. 20 Then when Martha heard that Jesus was coming, she went and met him, but Mary stayed in the house.

21 Therefore Martha said to Jesus, "Lord, if you would have been here, my brother wouldn't have died.

* * * * * * * * * * *

JIM'S THOUGHT FOR THE DAY

The question isn't "Have you ever second guessed God?", but "When is the last time you second guessed God?" We have all done it haven't we?

Despite our attempts to trust God's decisions and timing, we still are tempted to question his ways.

In this passage Martha wonders why Jesus had delayed coming immediately when he received word that Lazarus was sick. "If you would have been here, my brother would not have died." Later Mary would say the same words. Obviously the sisters had had this discussion before Jesus arrived.

Is it wrong to ask "Why?" regarding God' actions? I think it is not a question of right or wrong but a matter of dealing with our incomplete knowledge of God's plan and timing. Faith challenges us to accept that he knows best.

CHALLENGE: TO ACCEPT IN FAITH YHAT GOD KNOWS BEST AND THAT HIS TIMING IS ALWAYS PERFECT.

Prayer:

LORD, I want to accept your wisdom in all things. Help me to know you care for me. Amen.

DAILY DEVOTIONAL 40

Scripture Reading: John 11:22-27

I AM THE RESURRECTION AND THE LIFE

22 Even now I know that whatever you ask of God, God will give you."

23 Jesus said to her, "Your brother will rise again."

24 Martha said to him, "I know that he will rise again in the resurrection at the last day."

25 Jesus said to her, "I am the resurrection and the life. He who believes in me will still live, even if he dies. 26 Whoever lives and believes in me will never die.

Do you believe this?"

27 She said to him, "Yes, Lord. I have come to believe that you are the Christ, God's Son, he who comes into the world."

* * * * * * * * * * * * * *

JIM'S THOUGHT FOR THE DAY

THIS IS THE FIFTH "I Am..." saying of Jesus.
* I am the Bread of Life (John 6:35)
* I am the Light of the World (John 8:12)
* I am the Door (John 10:9)
* I am the Good Shepherd (John 10:11,14)
* I am the Resurrection and the Life (John 11:25)
* I am the Way and the Truth and the Life (John 14:6)
* I am the Vine (John 15:1,5)

It is a matter of life and death.

Over and over Jesus talks about life. "I came that they may have life, and may have it abundantly." John 10:10
Spiritual life assures that there will be no spiritual death. Physical death is a reality. "It is appointed for men to die once". Hebrew 9:27. But spiritual death is avoided by believing in Jesus.

"Jesus said to her, "I am the resurrection and the life. He who believes in me will still live, even if he dies. Whoever lives and believes in me will never die." vs25,26

This present life is often referred to as "the land of the living" but it would be more accurate to call it "the land of the dying."

Jesus concludes this conversation with a question: "Do you believe this?" And that is the ultimate question. Martha's response was "Yes, Lord. I have come to believe that you are the Christ, God's Son, he who comes into the world." vs. 27

CHALLENGE: TO KNOW THE JOY AND ASSURANCE THAT IN CHRIST WE CAN AND WILL LIVE FOREVER.

Prayer:

LORD, I thank you for being the resurrection and life. Amen.

DAILY DEVOTIONAL 41

Scripture Reading: John 11:28-44

JESUS WEPT

28 When she had said this, she went away and called Mary, her sister, secretly, saying, "The Teacher is here and is calling you."...

32 Therefore when Mary came to where Jesus was and saw him, she fell down at his feet, saying to him, "Lord, if you would have been here, my brother wouldn't have died."
33 When Jesus therefore saw her weeping, and the Jews weeping who came with her, he groaned in the spirit, and was troubled, 34 and said, "Where have you laid him?"
They told him, "Lord, come and see."

35 Jesus wept.

36 The Jews therefore said, "See how much affection he had for him!" 37 Some of them said, "Couldn't this man, who opened the eyes of him who was blind, have also kept this man from dying?"
38 Jesus therefore, again groaning in himself, came to the tomb. Now it was a cave, and a stone lay against it. 39 Jesus said, "Take away the stone."...

41 So they took away the stone from the place where the dead man was lying. Jesus lifted up his eyes, and said, "Father, I thank you that you listened to me. 42 I know that you always listen to me, but because of the multitude standing around I said this, that they may believe that you sent me." 43 When he had said this, he cried with a loud voice, "Lazarus, come out!"
44 He who was dead came out, bound hand and foot with wrappings, and his face was wrapped around with a cloth.
Jesus said to them, "Free him, and let him go."

* * * * * * * * * * * *

JIM'S THOUGHT FOR THE DAY

"Jesus wept." vs. 35

Though it is known as the shortest verse in the Bible, it is a large verse in meaning.

There are three times recorded in Scripture that Jesus wept (John 11:35; Luke 19:41; Hebrews 5:7-9). Each is near the end of His life and each reveals what matters most to our loving God. He truly is "touched with the feeling of our infirmities" (Hebrews 4:15). His tears are a reminder that He loves sinners and cares for every soul.

I have visited the Memorial in Oklahoma City several times that was erected on the site of the tragic bombing of the Federal Building on April 19, 1995. 168 people were killed and 650 others injured. Immediately across the street from the Memorial is a Catholic Church. On the corner the church erected a statue of Jesus showing his face in his hands and the words "Jesus wept."

"Oh, yes, He cares, I know He cares.
His heart is touched with my grief.
When the days are weary
The long night dreary
I know my Savior cares."

"Humble yourselves, therefore, under the mighty hand of God so that at the proper time he may exalt you, casting all your anxieties on him, because he cares for you." 1 Peter 5.6-7.

He loves. He cares. He weeps.

CHALLENGE: TO EXPERIENCE THE COMPASSIONATE LOVE OF JESUS EACH DAY IN EVERY CIRCUMSTANCE.

Prayer:

LORD, Thank you for caring "for a sinner such as I." Amen

DAILY DEVOTIONAL 42

Scripture Reading: John 11:45-57

DOING WHAT IS POLITICALLY CORRECT

45 Therefore many of the Jews who came to Mary and saw what Jesus did believed in him. 46 But some of them went away to the Pharisees and told them the things which Jesus had done. 47 The chief priests therefore and the Pharisees gathered a council, and said, "What are we doing? For this man does many signs. 48 If we leave him alone like this, everyone will believe in him, and the Romans will come and take away both our place and our nation."

49 But a certain one of them, Caiaphas, being high priest that year, said to them, "You know nothing at all, 50 nor do you consider that it is advantageous for us that one man should die for the people, and that the whole nation not perish." 51 Now he didn't say this of himself, but being high priest that year, he prophesied that Jesus would die for the nation, 52 and not for the nation only, but that he might also gather together into one the children of God who are scattered abroad. 53 So from that day forward they took counsel that they might put him to death. 54 Jesus therefore walked no more openly among the Jews, but departed from there into the country near the wilderness, to a city called Ephraim. He stayed there with his disciples.

55 Now the Passover of the Jews was at hand. Many went up from the country to Jerusalem before the Passover, to purify themselves. 56 Then they sought for Jesus and spoke with one another as they stood in the temple, "What do you think—that he isn't coming to the feast at all?" 57 Now the chief priests and the Pharisees had commanded that if anyone knew where he was, he should report it, that they might seize him.

* * * * * * * * * * * *

JIM'S THOUGHT FOR THE DAY

The expression "politically correct" is very common today. The expression may be recent but the practice of it is ancient.

The religious leaders of Jesus' day did what was politically correct in condemning Jesus. The Romans did what was politically correct in crucifying Him.

As followers of Jesus, you and I are challenged in our time to do what is morally and spiritually correct instead of what is politically correct. The downward spiral of the morals in our society is alarming.

Can you focus on something that we as Christians need to stand for that is not politically correct?

We need courage to stand for what is right. Compromise to please others or to fit in is not Christian. Silence is destructive when truth needs to be voiced. We must are more about what God thinks than what our friends/neighbors think. Is your desire to please God?

CHALLENGE: TO STAND UP AND SPEAK OUT IN OUR DARK SOCIETY STANDING FOR RIGHTEOUSNESS AND TRUTH.

Prayer:

LORD, Help me to have courage and strength to stand up and be counted! Amen

DAILY DEVOTIONAL 43

Scripture Reading: John 12:1-11

MARTHA SERVED, MARY ANOINTED

12:1 Then six days before the Passover, Jesus came to Bethany, where Lazarus was, who had been dead, whom he raised from the dead.

2 So they made him a supper there. Martha served, but Lazarus was one of those who sat at the table with him. 3 Therefore Mary took a pound of ointment of pure nard, very precious, and anointed Jesus's feet and wiped his feet with her hair. The house was filled with the fragrance of the ointment.

4 Then Judas Iscariot, Simon's son, one of his disciples, who would betray him, said, 5 "Why wasn't this ointment sold for three hundred denarii, and given to the poor?" 6 Now he said this, not because he cared for the poor, but because he was a thief, and having the money box, used to steal what was put into it.

7 But Jesus said, "Leave her alone. She has kept this for the day of my burial. 8 For you always have the poor with you, but you don't always have me."

9 A large crowd therefore of the Jews learned that he was there, and they came, not for Jesus' sake only, but that they might see Lazarus also, whom he had raised from the dead.

10 But the chief priests conspired to put Lazarus to death also, 11 because on account of him many of the Jews went away and believed in Jesus.

* * * * * * * * * * * * * * * *

JIM'S THOUGHT FOR THE DAY

Mary and Martha, along with their brother Lazarus, were special friends of Jesus. They lived in Bethany. Bethany was only a few miles from Jerusalem. Jesus stayed in Bethany at night during his last week before the crucifixion going to Jerusalem each day except on Wednesday. Jesus probably stayed in the home of these three friends.

"Martha served". vs. 2. Such a simple statement carries a lot of meaning. Martha was busy serving the Lord. She did not sit at the table and eat but served Jesus, Lazarus and others at the table.

"Mary took a pound of ointment of pure nard, very precious, and anointed Jesus's feet and wiped his feet with her hair." vs. 3. Her gift of pure nard, an aromatic amber-colored essential oil, was an expensive gift of love. The cost of three hundred denarii would probably have been close to $5,000 in our currency today.

Rosella Cook was a faithful member of our church. Some of you might have had the joy of knowing her. Like Martha she served. Like Mary she washed feet. No task was below her dignity. She would visit nursing homes and bath feet and give free pedicures to patients as an act of kindness and love. She found joy in helping other. She was a dear friend and I was inspired by her many acts of service and kindness. She was a great example of one who served.

I hope you have had some Marthas and Mary's in your life. I hope you and I might be a friend to people like Martha and Mary.

CHALLENGE: TO HAVE A SERVANTS HEART TOWARD JESUS AND OUR FELLOW MEN EXPRESSING WITH LOVE THAT WE CARE.

Prayer:

LORD, Help me find a way today to be kind, thoughtful and giving in Jesus' name. Amen

DAILY DEVOTIONAL 44

Scripture Reading: John 12:12-19

THE LORD, THE KING OF ISRAEL

12:12 On the next day a great multitude had come to the feast. When they heard that Jesus was coming to Jerusalem, 13 they took the branches of the palm trees and went out to meet him, and cried out, "Hosanna! Blessed is he who comes in the name of the Lord, the King of Israel!"

14 Jesus, having found a young donkey, sat on it. As it is written, 15 "Don't be afraid, daughter of Zion. Behold, your King comes, sitting on a donkey's colt." 16 His disciples didn't understand these things at first, but when Jesus was glorified, then they remembered that these things were written about him, and that they had done these things to him.

17 The multitude therefore that was with him when he called Lazarus out of the tomb and raised him from the dead was testifying about it. 18 For this cause also the multitude went and met him, because they heard that he had done this sign.

19 The Pharisees therefore said among themselves, "See how you accomplish nothing. Behold, the world has gone after him."

* * * * * * * * * * * *

JIM'S THOUGHT FOR THE DAY

"Hosanna! Blessed is he who comes in the name of the Lord, the King of Israel!" vs 13

I did not hear the term "King Jesus" as I was growing up in my church except with reference to the second coming.

I love the song "The King is Coming!" Bruce Forlines engraved that song in my heart many years ago. His recording of the song is still often used at funerals at our church.

"O the King is coming. The King is coming
I just heard the trumpets sounding, And now His face I see
O the King is coming, The King is coming
Praise God, He's coming for me."

Jesus is "King of Kings and Lord of Lords." Pilate had a sign placed on his cross, "King of the Jews". Perhaps Pilate was being sarcastic in doing so but the sign spoke a truth.

The so called "Triumphant Entry" into Jerusalem on Palm Sunday is often compared with the glorious return of Jesus prophesied in the Bible. "Oh, what a glorious day that will be."

Hail, King Jesus!

CHALLENGE: TO WORSHIP THE KING WITH AWE AND PRAISE KNOWING THAT THERE IS NONE OTHER LIKE HIM.

Prayer:

LORD, I come into your presence with amazement. You are worthy to be praised. Amen.

DAILY DEVOTIONAL 45

Scripture Reading: John 12:20-34

WE WANT TO SEE JESUS

20 Now there were certain Greeks among those who went up to worship at the feast. 21 These, therefore, came to Philip, who was from Bethsaida of Galilee, and asked him, saying, "Sir, we want to see Jesus." 22 Philip came and told Andrew, and in turn, Andrew came with Philip, and they told Jesus. 23 Jesus answered them, "The time has come for the Son of Man to be glorified. 24 Most certainly I tell you, unless a grain of wheat falls into the earth and dies, it remains by itself alone. But if it dies, it bears much fruit. 25 He who loves his life will lose it. He who hates his life in this world will keep it to eternal life. 26 If anyone serves me, let him follow me. Where I am, there my servant will also be. If anyone serves me, the Father will honor him.

27 "Now my soul is troubled. What shall I say? 'Father, save me from this time?' But I came to this time for this cause. 28 Father, glorify your name!"

Then a voice came out of the sky, saying, "I have both glorified it, and will glorify it again."

29 Therefore the multitude who stood by and heard it said that it had thundered. Others said, "An angel has spoken to him."

30 Jesus answered, "This voice hasn't come for my sake, but for your sakes. 31 Now is the judgment of this world. Now the prince of this world will be cast out. 32 And I, if I am lifted up from the earth, will draw all people to myself." 33 But he said this, signifying by what kind of death he should die. 34 The multitude answered him, "We have heard out of the law that the Christ remains forever. How do you say, 'The Son of Man must be lifted up?' Who is this Son of Man?"

* * * * * * * * * * * * * * * *

JIM'S THOUGHT FOR THE DAY

"We want to see Jesus." vs. 21

My first few sermons were preached in my home church. On the back side of the pulpit stand was a plaque with this verse: "We want to see Jesus." Seated on the platform before preaching, the words were a challenge to me. They have stayed with me through the years.

Of special note is the fact of who brought these Greek seekers to Jesus: Andrew and Phillip. Andrew was the brother of Simon Peter. He brought Peter to Jesus. He brought the young boy with loaves and fish to Jesus.

Most of us will think of someone who was instrumental in bring us to Jesus. How grateful we are for their influence and witness.

All around us are people who need to see Jesus. "People need the Lord".

"People need the Lord, people need the Lord
At the end of broken dreams, He's the open door...
When will we realize people need the Lord?"

CHALLENGE: TO BE SENSITIVE TO THE SPIRITUAL NEEDS OF PEOPLE ALL AROUND US AND BE READY TO BRING THEM TO JESUS.

Prayer:

LORD, Give me the courage to witness to other of your grace and power to save. Amen.

DAILY DEVOTIONAL 46

Scripture Reading: John 12:35-50

THE LIGHT OF THE WORLD IS JESUS

35 Jesus therefore said to them, "Yet a little while the light is with you. Walk while you have the light, that darkness doesn't overtake you. He who walks in the darkness doesn't know where he is going. 36 While you have the light, believe in the light, that you may become children of light."

Jesus said these things, and he departed and hid himself from them. 37 But though he had done so many signs before them, yet they didn't believe in him, 38 that the word of Isaiah the prophet might be fulfilled, which he spoke,
"Lord, who has believed our report? To whom has the arm of the Lord been revealed?" ...

... 44 Jesus cried out and said, "Whoever believes in me, believes not in me, but in him who sent me. 45 He who sees me sees him who sent me. 46 I have come as a light into the world, that whoever believes in me may not remain in the darkness. 47 If anyone listens to my sayings, and doesn't believe, I don't judge him. For I came not to judge the world, but to save the world.

48 He who rejects me, and doesn't receive my sayings, has one who judges him. The word that I spoke will judge him in the last day. 49 For I spoke not from myself, but the Father who sent me, he gave me a commandment, what I should say, and what I should speak.

50 I know that his commandment is eternal life. The things therefore which I speak, even as the Father has said to me, so I speak."

* * * * * * * * * * * * * *

JIM'S THOUGHT FOR THE DAY

Jesus said: "I have come as a light into the world, that whoever believes in me may not remain in the darkness." vs. 46

Again Jesus uses the analogy of light and darkness to explain his purpose and plan.

In the Bible, light has always been a symbol of holiness, goodness, knowledge, wisdom, grace, hope, and God's revelation. By contrast, darkness has been associated with evil, sin, and despair.

John begins his gospel: "In him was life, and the life was the light of men. The light shines in the darkness, and the darkness hasn't overcome it." John 1:4,5

He gives sight to a blind man as a sign of light.

He says specifically, "I am the light of the world". John 8:12.

"The light of the world is Jesus."

I cannot imagine living without light. I am thankful I do not live in spiritual darkness.

CHALLENGE: TO FOLLOW THE ONE WHO IS THE LIGHT OF THE WORLD.

Prayer:

LORD, I ask you to light my path as I take life's journey. Amen.

DAILY DEVOTIONAL 47

Scripture Reading: John 13:1-20

DOING THE TASK OF A SERVANT

13 Now before the feast of the Passover, Jesus, knowing that his time had come that he would depart from this world to the Father, having loved his own who were in the world, he loved them to the end. 2 During supper, the devil having already put into the heart of Judas Iscariot, Simon's son, to betray him, 3 Jesus, knowing that the Father had given all things into his hands, and that he came from God, and was going to God, 4 arose from supper, and laid aside his outer garments. He took a towel and wrapped a towel around his waist. 5 Then he poured water into the basin, and began to wash the disciples' feet and to wipe them with the towel that was wrapped around him. 6 Then he came to Simon Peter. He said to him, "Lord, do you wash my feet?"

7 Jesus answered him, "You don't know what I am doing now, but you will understand later."

8 Peter said to him, "You will never wash my feet!"

Jesus answered him, "If I don't wash you, you have no part with me."

9 Simon Peter said to him, "Lord, not my feet only, but also my hands and my head!"

10 Jesus said to him, "Someone who has bathed only needs to have his feet washed, but is completely clean. You are clean, but not all of you." 11 For he knew him who would betray him, therefore he said, "You are not all clean." 12 So when he had washed their feet, put his outer garment back on, and sat down again, he said to them, "Do you know what I have done to you? 13 You call me, 'Teacher' and 'Lord.' You say so correctly, for so I am. 14 If I then, the Lord and the Teacher, have washed your feet, you also ought to wash one another's feet. ..."

* * * * * * * * * * * *

JIM'S THOUGHT FOR THE DAY

"He...began to wash the disciples' feet." vs.5

Jesus not only took on the form of a servant, he performed the task of a servant. The disciples were amazed. Simon Peter's response was that he would not allow Jesus to wash his feet. But Jesus taught him a spiritual lesson. Being cleansed by Jesus is essential.

In my childhood community there was a "foot washing Baptist Church". As a part of worship they literally washed one another feet. The early Christian church did not understand that foot washing was meant to be an ordinance like the taking of the bread and the cup in the Lord's Supper.

However there is a principle here that must not be missed. The principle of humility and servitude is illustrated by this act of Jesus. The washing of feet is an example of spiritual cleansing. Recognizing this Peter said, "Lord, not my feet only, but also my hands and my head!"

So this experience of the disciple's teaches us to be humble servants and cleansed followers of Jesus.

CHALLENGE: TO HUMBLE OURSELVES BEFORE GOD AND BEFORE OUR FELLOWMEN AS SERVANTS OF ALL.

Prayer:

LORD, I am not worthy of your grace. Help me to be your servant in the world. Amen.

DAILY DEVOTIONAL 48

Scripture Reading: John 13:21-38

A NEW COMMANDMENT: LOVE ONE ANOTHER

21 When Jesus had said this, he was troubled in spirit, and testified, "Most certainly I tell you that one of you will betray me."
22 The disciples looked at one another, perplexed about whom he spoke. 23 One of his disciples, whom Jesus loved, was at the table, leaning against Jesus' breast. 24 Simon Peter therefore beckoned to him, and said to him, "Tell us who it is of whom he speaks."
25 He, leaning back, as he was, on Jesus' breast, asked him, "Lord, who is it?"
26 Jesus therefore answered, "It is he to whom I will give this piece of bread when I have dipped it." So when he had dipped the piece of bread, he gave it to Judas, the son of Simon Iscariot. 27 After the piece of bread, then Satan entered into him.
Then Jesus said to him, "What you do, do quickly."
28 Now nobody at the table knew why he said this to him. 29 For some thought, because Judas had the money box, that Jesus said to him, "Buy what things we need for the feast," or that he should give something to the poor. 30 Therefore having received that morsel, he went out immediately. It was night.
31 When he had gone out, Jesus said, "Now the Son of Man has been glorified, and God has been glorified in him. 32 If God has been glorified in him, God will also glorify him in himself, and he will glorify him immediately. 33 Little children, I will be with you a little while longer. You will seek me, and as I said to the Jews, 'Where I am going, you can't come,' so now I tell you.

34 A new commandment I give to you, that you love one another. Just as I have loved you, you also love one another. 35 By this everyone will know that you are my disciples, if you have love for one another." ...

* * * * * * * * * * * *

JIM'S THOUGHT FOR THE DAY

Jesus said, "Just as I have loved you, you also love one another."

It sounds so simple. But it is so profound. And Jesus makes it plan that this commandment is not optional. This is the way we show and prove that we are his disciples.

I once heard a popular preacher say that the most neglected principle of the Bible is the judgement of God. While I believe in the judgment of God, I believe the most neglected principle of the Bible is love.

We use the word love so loosely. We love God and we love ice cream.
In the Bible there are three different words translated love.
* Eros: Sexual passion. ...(erotic)
* Philia: Deep friendship. ... (Philadelphia, the city of brotherly love.)
* Agape: Love for everyone. ... (John 3:16 love)
The word Jesus uses here is Agape. It is the word used throughout John' gospel to express God's love to us and our love to God and our fellow men. It is a pure, unselfish and unlimited affection and devotion.

We continue to see the importance of agape love in the teachings of Jesus. The continuing repetitions emphasize the importance of love. Love is the basis of meaningful relationships. Love is the proof of true discipleship.

CHALLENGE: TO LOVE IN SUCH A WAY THOSE OTHERS WILL KNOW WE ARE DISCIPLES OF JESUS.

Prayer:

LORD: I love you. I want to be a demonstration of your love by showing my love to others. Amen.

DAILY DEVOTIONAL 49

Scripture Reading: John 14:1-14

THE WAY, THE TRUTH, AND THE LIFE

14:1. "Don't let your heart be troubled. Believe in God. Believe also in me. 2 In my Father's house are many homes. If it weren't so, I would have told you. I am going to prepare a place for you. 3 If I go and prepare a place for you, I will come again, and will receive you to myself; that where I am, you may be there also. 4 You know where I go, and you know the way."
5 Thomas said to him, "Lord, we don't know where you are going. How can we know the way?

6 Jesus said to him, "I am the way, the truth, and the life. No one comes to the Father, except through me. 7 If you had known me, you would have known my Father also. From now on, you know him, and have seen him."
8 Philip said to him, "Lord, show us the Father, and that will be enough for us."
9 Jesus said to him, "Have I been with you such a long time, and do you not know me, Philip? He who has seen me has seen the Father. How do you say, 'Show us the Father?' 10 Don't you believe that I am in the Father, and the Father in me? The words that I tell you, I speak not from myself; but the Father who lives in me does his works.

11 Believe me that I am in the Father, and the Father in me; or else believe me for the very works' sake. 12 Most certainly I tell you, he who believes in me, the works that I do, he will do also; and he will do greater works than these, because I am going to my Father. 13 Whatever you will ask in my name, I will do it, that the Father may be glorified in the Son. 14 If you will ask anything in my name, I will do it.

* * * * * * * * * * * * * * * * *

JIM'S THOUGHT FOR THE DAY

"I am the way, the truth, and the life. vs. 6

This is the sixth of the seven "I am..." saying of Jesus:
* I am the Bread of Life (John 6:35)
* I am the Light of the World (John 8:12)
* I am the Door (John 10:9)
* I am the Good Shepherd (John 10:11, 14)
* I am the Resurrection and the Life (John 11:25)
* I am the Way and the Truth and the Life (John 14:6)
* I am the Vine (John 15:1, 5)

It is important to note that this passage is in the context of the Upper Room at Passover time. Jesus is trying to prepare his disciples for the crucifixion event. The time is at hand.

The truths of this saying are fundamental to the gospel. I know one pastor who always used this passage at a funeral. The words are the basis for our eternal hope.

Meditate on this verse today for fulfillment and joy in the good news. He is the way, the truth and the life. And remember you cannot come to the Father except through Him.

CHALLENGE: TO FIND SECURITY IN JESUS THAT ASSURES US OF A PLACE HE HAS PREPARED FOR US.

Prayer:

LORD, Thank you for showing me the way to eternal life.

DAILY DEVOTIONAL 50

Scripture Reading: John 14:15-21

BECAUSE HE LIVES

14:15 If you love me, keep my commandments.

16 I will pray to the Father, and he will give you another Counselor, that he may be with you forever: 17 the Spirit of truth, whom the world can't receive; for it doesn't see him and doesn't know him. You know him, for he lives with you, and will be in you.

18 I will not leave you orphans. I will come to you. 19 Yet a little while, and the world will see me no more; but you will see me. Because I live, you will live also.

20 In that day you will know that I am in my Father, and you in me, and I in you.

21 One who has my commandments and keeps them, that person is one who loves me. One who loves me will be loved by my Father, and I will love him, and will reveal myself to him."

* * * * * * * * * * * * * * * *

JIM'S THOUGHT FOR THE DAY

"Because I live, you will live also." vs. 19

Notice that the teachings about love continue in this passage. Also the emphasis on obedience. Jesus also emphasizes the importance of the Counselor. We will think about that tomorrow.

Also the emphasis on life and death is made once again. The cross is not about death but about the providing of life for those who believe.

The resurrection of Jesus is the basis of our faith. Paul writes in I Corinthians 15:

"12 Now if Christ is preached, that he has been raised from the dead, how do some among you say that there is no resurrection of the dead? 13 But if there is no resurrection of the dead, neither has Christ been raised. 14 If Christ has not been raised, then our preaching is in vain, and your faith also is in vain. ... 17 If Christ has not been raised, your faith is vain; you are still in your sins. 18 Then they also who are fallen asleep in Christ have perished. 19 If we have only hoped in Christ in this life, we are of all men most pitiable."

"Because He lives I can face tomorrow.
Because He lives all fear is gone.
Because I know He holds the future.
And life is worth the living, Just because He lives."

CHALLENGE: TO HOLD ON TO THE HISTORIC REALITY OF THE RESURRECTION WITH ASSURANCE THAT HE IS ALIVE!

Prayer:

LORD, I thank you for your power over death and the grave and rejoice in eternal life. Amen.

DAILY DEVOTIONAL 51

Scripture Reading: John 14:22-32

THE COUNSELOR, THE HOLY SPIRIT, WILL TEACH YOU ALL THINGS

22 Judas (not Iscariot) said to him, "Lord, what has happened that you are about to reveal yourself to us, and not to the world?"

23 Jesus answered him, "If a man loves me, he will keep my word. My Father will love him, and we will come to him, and make our home with him. 24 He who doesn't love me doesn't keep my words. The word which you hear isn't mine, but the Father's who sent me.

25 I have said these things to you while still living with you. 26 But the Counselor, the Holy Spirit, whom the Father will send in my name, will teach you all things, and will remind you of all that I said to you.

27 Peace I leave with you. My peace I give to you; not as the world gives, I give to you. Don't let your heart be troubled, neither let it be fearful. 28 You heard how I told you, 'I go away, and I come to you.' If you loved me, you would have rejoiced, because I said 'I am going to my Father;' for the Father is greater than I.

29 Now I have told you before it happens so that when it happens, you may believe. 30 I will no more speak much with you, for the prince of the world comes, and he has nothing in me.

31 But that the world may know that I love the Father, and as the Father commanded me, even so I do. Arise, let's go from here."

* * * * * * * * * * * * * * * *

JIM'S THOUGHT FOR THE DAY

As Jesus prepares his disciples for the events of the crucifixion/resurrection/ascension he gives them the promise that the Holy Spirit will be with them after he has returned to the Father. He refers to the Holy Spirit as the "Parakeet" (Comforter).

The word "Paraclete" is translated as Comforter, Advocate, Helper, Sustainer, Strengthener, Intercessor, Companion, Standby.

In the Christian New Testament, Paraclete appears only in the writings of John and it is used only on five occasions: Gospel of John 14:16, 14:26, 15:26, 16:7, and First Epistle of John chapter 2, verse 1.

Jesus gives his disciples a special promise. He assures them that they will not be left without help. A Helper will be with them. They will "not be orphans". John 14:18

"Be strong and courageous. Do not be afraid or terrified because of them, for the LORD your God goes with you; he will never leave you or forsake you".

The Paraclete enables us.

The Paraclete gives us peace. "My peace I give to you. ...Don't let your heart be troubled, neither let it be fearful." vs. 27

CHALLENGE: TO FIND COMFORT AND PEACE IN THE PRESENCE OF THE HOLY SPIRIT KNOWING THAT HE IS WITH ME.

Prayer:

LORD, I claim your promise and place myself in your enabling hands. Thank you for being my Comforter, Advocate, Helper, Sustainer, Strengthener, Intercessor, Companion, Standby.
Amen.

DAILY DEVOTIONAL 52

Scripture Reading: John 15:1-11

BEARING FRUIT FROM THE TRUE VINE

15:1 "I am the true vine, and my Father is the farmer. 2 Every branch in me that doesn't bear fruit, he takes away. Every branch that bears fruit, he prunes, that it may bear more fruit. 3 You are already pruned clean because of the word which I have spoken to you.

4 Remain in me, and I in you. As the branch can't bear fruit by itself unless it remains in the vine, so neither can you, unless you remain in me. 5 I am the vine. You are the branches. He who remains in me and I in him bears much fruit, for apart from me you can do nothing. 6 If a man doesn't remain in me, he is thrown out as a branch and is withered; and they gather them, throw them into the fire, and they are burned.

7 If you remain in me, and my words remain in you, you will ask whatever you desire, and it will be done for you.
8 "In this my Father is glorified, that you bear much fruit; and so you will be my disciples."

9 Even as the Father has loved me, I also have loved you. Remain in my love. 10 If you keep my commandments, you will remain in my love; even as I have kept my Father's commandments, and remain in his love.

11 I have spoken these things to you, that my joy may remain in you, and that your joy may be made full."

* * * * * * * * * *

JIM'S THOUGHT FOR THE DAY

This is the last of the seven "I Am ..." sayings of Jesus found in John's Gospel: "I am the true vine." vs. 1

The source of fruit is in the vine. What does it mean to bear fruit as a follower of Jesus?

The Fruit of the Holy Spirit is a biblical term that sums up nine attributes of a person or community living in accord with the Holy Spirit, according to chapter 5 of the Epistle to the Galatians: "But the fruit of the Spirit is love, joy, peace, patience, kindness, goodness, faithfulness, gentleness, and self-control.

These fruits describe the character of Jesus. When we bear these fruits we are like him.

Followers of Jesus are not just followers in words only. While we confess him with our mouths, we emulate Him in our lives and in our character. We grow in Christ likeness.

To not bear fruit is an indication that we are not connected to Him.

Producing these fruits brings us joy! vs. 11.

CHALLENGE: TO PRODUCE THE FRUITS OF THE SPIRIT IN ABUNDANCE AS I REMAIN CONNECTED TO THE TRUE VINE.

Prayer:

LORD, I want to become more and more like you day by day. Give me the strength to be faithful. Amen.

DAILY DEVOTIONAL 53

Scripture Reading: John 15:12-27

HE IS YOUR BEST FRIEND

15:12 "This is my commandment, that you love one another, even as I have loved you. 13 Greater love has no one than this, that someone lay down his life for his friends. 14 You are my friends, if you do whatever I command you. 15 No longer do I call you servants, for the servant doesn't know what his lord does. But I have called you friends, for everything that I heard from my Father, I have made known to you.

16 You didn't choose me, but I chose you and appointed you, that you should go and bear fruit, and that your fruit should remain; that whatever you will ask of the Father in my name, he may give it to you. 17 "I command these things to you, that you may love one another. ...

... 23 He who hates me, hates my Father also. 24 If I hadn't done among them the works which no one else did, they wouldn't have had sin. But now they have seen and also hated both me and my Father. 25 But this happened so that the word may be fulfilled which was written in their law, 'They hated me without a cause.'

26 "When the Counselor has come, whom I will send to you from the Father, the Spirit of truth, who proceeds from the Father, he will testify about me. 27 You will also testify, because you have been with me from the beginning."

* * * * * * * * * * * * * * * *

JIM'S THOUGHT FOR THE DAY

"No longer do I call you servants, ...But I have called you friends." vs. 15.

Notice again the continuing emphasis on the command to love one another. Jesus also continues talking about the principle of bearing fruit in our lives.

But I want us to focus today on: "I have called you friends".

Have you heard someone refer to their "Bestie"? A Bestie is simply a best friend. My life has been blessed with good friends. Several best friends have brought joy and special meaning to my life. One famous person said, "I would rather have one hundred friends than a million dollars."

But Jesus is a friend like no other.

The gospel song says:
"What a friend we have in Jesus, All our sins and griefs to bear. And what a privilege to carry, Everything to God in prayer."

You enjoy spending time with a friend. You like talking with a friend.

I hope you are blessed with good friends. I hope that your best friend is Jesus. "He walks with me and he talks with me, and he tells me I am his own."

CHALLENGE: TO HAVE A CLOSE RELATIONSHIP WITH JESUS KNOWING HIM AS A FRIEND INDEED.

Prayer:

LORD, I want to be your friend in love and devotion. Amen.

DAILY DEVOTIONAL 54

Scripture Reading: John 16:1-11

THE COUNSELOR AT WORK FOR YOU

16:1 "I have said these things to you so that you wouldn't be caused to stumble. 2 They will put you out of the synagogues. Yes, the time comes that whoever kills you will think that he offers service to God.

3 They will do these things because they have not known the Father, nor me. 4 But I have told you these things, so that when the time comes, you may remember that I told you about them. I didn't tell you these things from the beginning, because I was with you.

5 But now I am going to him who sent me, and none of you asks me, 'Where are you going?' 6 But because I have told you these things, sorrow has filled your heart.

7 Nevertheless I tell you the truth: It is to your advantage that I go away, for if I don't go away, the Counselor won't come to you. But if I go, I will send him to you.

8 When he has come, he will convict the worldwide about sin, about righteousness, and about judgment;

9 about sin, because they don't believe in me; 10 about righteousness, because I am going to my Father, and you won't see me any more; 11 about judgment, because the prince of this world has been judged.

* * * * * * * * * * * *

JIM'S THOUGHT FOR THE DAY

Jesus helps his followers understand the work of the Counselor (Holy Spirit). Over and over Jesus has emphasized that he and the Father are one. Now he wants his followers to understand that the work of the Holy Spirit is also one with Him and the Father.

The Holy Spirit will not be limited by time or space. Jesus says the Spirit will be able to do even greater works that He.

"When he has come, he will convict the worldwide about sin, about righteousness, and about judgment". vs. 8

We need to face the truth about sin. If a Medical Doctor did not tell us the truth about a physical illness, he would not be doing us a favor but a serious disservice. We need the conviction of sin given by the Holy Spirit in order to cultivate the fruits of the Spirit.

The Holy Spirit confirms the word of Jesus. He brings conviction of truth over sin. He pronounces victory over the prince of this world. One theologian refers to the Holy Spirit as the "other Jesus".

There is a complete consistency between the work and the words of the Father, the Son and the Holy Spirit.

The Holy Spirit is our Helper.

CHALLENGE: TO LET THE HOLY SPIRIT CONVICT ME OF SIN, RIGHTEOUSNESS AND JUDGMENT.

Prayer:

LORD, Thank you for the Spirit of Truth that is my teacher in all things. Amen.

DAILY DEVOTIONAL 55

Scripture Reading; John 16:12-22

YOUR SORROW WILL BE TURNED TO JOY

16:12. I have yet many things to tell you, but you can't bear them now. 13However when he, the Spirit of truth, has come, he will guide you into all truth, for he will not speak from himself; but whatever he hears, he will speak. He will declare to you things that are coming. 14He will glorify me, for he will take from what is mine, and will declare it to you. 15All things whatever the Father has are mine; therefore I said that he takes of mine, and will declare it to you.

16A little while, and you will not see me. Again a little while, and you will see me."

17Some of his disciples therefore said to one another, "What is this that he says to us, 'A little while, and you won't see me, and again a little while, and you will see me;' and, 'Because I go to the Father?'" 18They said therefore, "What is this that he says, 'A little while?' We don't know what he is saying." 19Therefore Jesus perceived that they wanted to ask him, and he said to them, "Do you inquire among yourselves concerning this, that I said, 'A little while, and you won't see me, and again a little while, and you will see me?'

20Most certainly I tell you, that you will weep and lament, but the world will rejoice. You will be sorrowful, but your sorrow will be turned into joy. 21A woman, when she gives birth, has sorrow, because her time has come. But when she has delivered the child, she doesn't remember the anguish any more, for the joy that a human being is born into the world. 22Therefore you now have sorrow, but I will see you again, and your heart will rejoice, and no one will take your joy away from you.

* * * * * * * * * * * * *

JIM'S THOUGHT FOR THE DAY

Jesus continues to prepare his disciples for his death and departure. They are concerned about what will happen when he is no longer with them.

He has promised them that the Holy Spirit will be with them. The Holy Spirit will be their Comforter, their Sustainer, their Helper, etc.

Jesus uses the example of a woman giving birth. Her birth pains give way to joy with the coming of the baby. So the disciples' hurt and sorrow will be overcome with the joy of the blessings of God.

Jesus promises them a joy that cannot be taken away from them.

A popular youth chorus says:
"If you want joy, real joy, wonderful joy, Let Jesus come into your heart.
Your sins he'll take away, your night he'll turn to day. Let Jesus come into your heart."

Jesus turns our sorrows into joy.

Jesus uses the term "the Spirit of Truth" in reference to the Holy Spirit. He will guide us.

CHALLENGE: TO KNOW THAT I AM PROVIDED FOR BY ONE WHO CAN TURN MY NIGHTS INTO DAYS AND HELP ME OVERCOME THE SORROWS OF LIFE

Prayer:

LORD, I pray that I might receive the Holy Spirit with joy and satisfaction. Amen.

DAILY DEVOTIONAL 56

Scripture Reading: John 16:23-33

CHEER UP! I HAVE OVERCOME THE WORLD

16:23. In that day you will ask me no questions. Most certainly I tell you, whatever you may ask of the Father in my name, he will give it to you. 24Until now, you have asked nothing in my name. Ask, and you will receive, that your joy may be made full.

25I have spoken these things to you in figures of speech. But the time is coming when I will no more speak to you in figures of speech, but will tell you plainly about the Father. 26In that day you will ask in my name; and I don't say to you, that I will pray to the Father for you, 27for the Father himself loves you, because you have loved me, and have believed that I came forth from God. 28I came out from the Father, and have come into the world. Again, I leave the world, and go to the Father."

29His disciples said to him, "Behold, now you speak plainly, and speak no figures of speech. 30Now we know that you know all things, and don't need for anyone to question you. By this we believe that you came forth from God."

31Jesus answered them, "Do you now believe? 32Behold, the time is coming, yes, and has now come, that you will be scattered, everyone to his own place, and you will leave me alone. Yet I am not alone, because the Father is with me.

33I have told you these things, that in me you may have peace. In the world you have oppression; but cheer up! I have overcome the world.

* * * * * * * * * * * *

JIM'S THOUGHT FOR THE DAY

"Cheer up!" Those are often empty words. Well intended people often give that advise without understanding the problems being faced. Real answers are needed for real problems, not just a pep talk.

But Jesus gives us reasons why we can cheer up.

Because He promises answers to our prayers. "Ask of the Father in my name, he will give it to you". vs. 23

Because He assures us that God loves us. "For the Father himself loves you." vs. 27

Because our faith will be fulfilled in knowing that Jesus came from the Father. vs. 28

Because He gives us peace in the midst of difficulties. "...in me you may have peace". vs. 33

Because He has overcome the world. vs. 33

Jesus says, "Cheer up!" His words give us assurance.

CHALLENGE: TO BE OF GOOD CHEER REGARDLESS OF THE CIRCUMSTANCES OF LIFE FOR HE HAS OVERCOME THE WORLD.

Prayer:

LORD, I thank you for the many reasons I can be of good cheer. Help me to express my joy to others. Amen

DAILY DEVOTIONAL 57

Scripture Reading: John 17:1-19

JESUS PRAYS FOR YOU

17:1 Jesus said these things, and lifting up his eyes to heaven, he said, "Father, the time has come. Glorify your Son, that your Son may also glorify you; 2even as you gave him authority over all flesh, he will give eternal life to all whom you have given him. 3This is eternal life, that they should know you, the only true God, and him whom you sent, Jesus Christ. 4I glorified you on the earth. I have accomplished the work which you have given me to do. 5Now, Father, glorify me with your own self with the glory which I had with you before the world existed.

6I revealed your name to the people whom you have given me out of the world. They were yours, and you have given them to me. They have kept your word. 7Now they have known that all things whatever you have given me are from you, 8for the words which you have given me I have given to them, and they received them, and knew for sure that I came forth from you, and they have believed that you sent me. 9I pray for them. I don't pray for the world, but for those whom you have given me, for they are yours. 10All things that are mine are yours, and yours are mine, and I am glorified in them. ...

...13 But now I come to you, and I say these things in the world, that they may have my joy made full in themselves. 14 I have given them your word. The world hated them, because they are not of the world, even as I am not of the world. 15 I pray not that you would take them from the world, but that you would keep them from the evil one. 16 They are not of the world even as I am not of the world. 17 Sanctify them in your truth. Your word is truth. 18 As you sent me into the world, even so I have sent them into the world. 19 For their sakes I sanctify myself, that they themselves also may be sanctified in truth.

* * * * * * * * * * *

JIM'S THOUGHT FOR THE DAY

"I'm praying for you." Those are special words for encouragement. It is great to know people are praying for us.

Nannie B. was one of God's wonderful saints. She was a blessing to me in my young ministry. She encouraged me in many ways. One day she said to me, "Brother Jim, I pray for you every day." I knew she did. She blessed me with her prayers.

In your time of special need, who would you want to be praying for you? I can name some devoted people I want praying for me. I think you can too.

And you and I need to be praying faithfully for one another and for others. Prayer changes things. Prayer changes others. Prayer changes me. Prayer changes you.

Remember, Jesus prays for you! He keeps you. vs. 12. Isn't that an amazing truth! He says, "I pray for them." vs. 9

He keeps us from the evil one. vs. 15

He sanctifies is (keeps us pure) in the truth. vs. 19

CHALLENGE: TO FIND CONFIDENCE IN KNOWING THAT JESUS PRAYS FOR ME.

Prayer:

LORD, Your prayers sustain and encourage me. Thank you for knowing and loving me. Amen.

DAILY DEVOTIONAL 58

Scripture Reading: John 17:20-26

THE LORD'S PRAYER:
FOR HIS FOLLOWERS TO BE ONE

17:20 Not for these only do I pray, but for those also who believe in me through their word, 21that they may all be one; even as you, Father, are in me, and I in you, that they also may be one in us; that the world may believe that you sent me.

22The glory which you have given me, I have given to them; that they may be one, even as we are one; 23I in them, and you in me, that they may be perfected into one; that the world may know that you sent me, and loved them, even as you loved me.

24Father, I desire that they also whom you have given me be with me where I am, that they may see my glory, which you have given me, for you loved me before the foundation of the world.

25Righteous Father, the world hasn't known you, but I knew you; and these knew that you sent me. 26I made known to them your name, and will make it known; that the love with which you loved me may be in them, and I in them.

* * * * * * * * * * * *

JIM'S THOUGHT FOR THE DAY

THE LORD'S PRAYER

The prayer that begins: "Our Father, who art in Heaven, hallowed be your name ..." is commonly referred to as The Lord's Prayer. Jesus gave this prayer to the disciples after they ask Him, "Teach us to pray ". Luke 11. It might be more accurate to call it the Disciple's Prayer.

The entirety of John, chapter 17, is a prayer.

The prayer given here can rightfully be referred to as the Lord's Prayer. After praying for the disciples in the first part of the chapter, Jesus then prays for himself.

He prays, "... that the world may know that You sent me." vs. 23

He prays, "... that the world may know that you loved them ... even as you loved me." vs. 23

He prays, "... that they may see my glory." vs. 24

Jesus prayed to God because God infused him with a spirit of prayer and also because of who Christ is in relation to his Father, namely, the Son of God. His identity, coupled with God's own desire to commune with his Son, explain why Jesus needed to pray.

CHALLENGE: TO FOLLOW THE EXAMPLE OF JESUS IN PRAYER.

Prayer:

LORD, I thank you for teaching me how to pray in faith. Amen.

DAILY DEVOTIONAL 59

Scripture Reading: John 18:1-11

WHO ARE YOU LOOKING FOR?

18:1 When Jesus had spoken these words, he went out with his disciples over the brook Kidron, where there was a garden, into which he and his disciples entered.

2Now Judas, who betrayed him, also knew the place, for Jesus often met there with his disciples. 3Judas then, having taken a detachment of soldiers and officers from the chief priests and the Pharisees, came there with lanterns, torches, and weapons.

4Jesus therefore, knowing all the things that were happening to him, went forth, and said to them, "Who are you looking for?" 5They answered him, "Jesus of Nazareth." Jesus said to them, "I am he." Judas also, who betrayed him, was standing with them. 6When therefore he said to them, "I am he," they went backward, and fell to the ground.

7Again therefore he asked them, "Who are you looking for?" They said, "Jesus of Nazareth." 8Jesus answered, "I told you that I am he. If therefore you seek me, let these go their way," 9that the word might be fulfilled which he spoke, "Of those whom you have given me, I have lost none."

10Simon Peter therefore, having a sword, drew it, and struck the high priest's servant, and cut off his right ear. The servant's name was Malchus.

11Jesus therefore said to Peter, "Put the sword into its sheath. The cup which the Father has given me, shall I not surely drink it?"

* * * * * * * * * * *

JIM'S THOUGHT FOR THE DAY

One of the problems the religious people of Jesus' day had is found in this question: "Who are you looking for?"

They were looking for Jesus of Nazareth. They were looking for a Messiah to become the King of Israel and rid them of Roman rule.

When they realized that Jesus was not going to be a political/military ruler, they stopped following him and turned on him.

Jesus plainly said, "My kingdom is not of this world."

Who are you looking for? Many religious people today are looking for a Jesus who will grant their every request. Some are looking for one who promises health and wealth. Others want a "feel good" giver.

In contrast Jesus offers a life of discipline. A life based on love. A life that puts others first. A life that sacrifices. A life of oneness with God.

Jesus did not hesitate to identify himself to those who would seize him. He faced the event of his death with resolution. His time was at hand. He was ready to complete the task.

CHALLENGE: TO ACCEPT THE REAL JESUS IN FAITH AND COMMITMENT.

Prayer:

LORD, I want to follow you as you ask me to do. Amen.

DAILY DEVOTIONAL 60

Scripture Reading: John 18:12-27

ARE YOU ONE OF HIS DISCIPLES?

18:12 The detachment, the commanding officer, and the officers of the Jews, seized Jesus and bound him, 13and led him to Annas first, for he was father-in-law to Caiaphas, who was high priest that year. 14Now it was Caiaphas who advised the Jews that it was expedient that one man should perish for the people.

15Simon Peter followed Jesus, as did another disciple. Now that disciple was known to the high priest, and entered in with Jesus into the court of the high priest; 16but Peter was standing at the door outside. So the other disciple, who was known to the high priest, went out and spoke to her who kept the door, and brought in Peter. 17Then the maid who kept the door said to Peter, "Are you also one of this man's disciples?" He said, "I am not." 18Now the servants and the officers were standing there, having made a fire of coals, for it was cold. They were warming themselves. Peter was with them, standing and warming himself. 19The high priest therefore asked Jesus about his disciples, and about his teaching. ...

...22When he had said this, one of the officers standing by slapped Jesus with his hand, saying, "Do you answer the high priest like that?" 23Jesus answered him, "If I have spoken evil, testify of the evil; but if well, why do you beat me?" 24Annas sent him bound to Caiaphas, the 25Now Simon Peter was standing and warming himself. They said therefore to him, "You aren't also one of his disciples, are you?" He denied it, and said, "I am not." 26One of the servants of the high priest, being a relative of him whose ear Peter had cut off, said, "Didn't I see you in the garden with him?" 27Peter therefore denied it again, and immediately the rooster crowed.

* * * * * * * * * * * * *

JIM'S THOUGHT FOR THE DAY

"Are you also one of this man's disciples? vs. 17

Peter had been brash in his declaration that he would never deny Jesus. This passage records the failure of Peter to live up to his promise. As Jesus predicted he denied him three times "before the cock crowed".

It is easy to find fault with Peter. There are lessons to be learned from his failure.

There are many ways we deny our relationship with Jesus. By our language. By our attitude. By our conduct. By our hate. By our criticisms.

Are there people who would be surprised to learn that you claim to be a follower of Jesus?

Jesus needs followers whose lives and words are a positive witness of who He is and what he can do.

Paul warns us: "Therefore let him who thinks he stands be careful that he doesn't fall." I Corinthians 10:12

CHALLENGE: TO BEAR A POSITIVE AND CONSISTENT WITNESS THAT I AM A FOLLOWER OF JESUS.

Prayer:

LORD, I want to be faithful to you and never be ashamed to testify to your grace and mercy. Amen.

DAILY DEVOTIONAL 61

Scripture Reading: John 18:28-40

WHAT IS TRUTH?

17:28 They led Jesus therefore from Caiaphas into the Praetorium. It was early, and they themselves didn't enter into the Praetorium, that they might not be defiled, but might eat the Passover. 29Pilate therefore went out to them, and said, "What accusation do you bring against this man?" 30They answered him, "If this man weren't an evildoer, we wouldn't have delivered him up to you." 31Pilate therefore said to them, "Take him yourselves, and judge him according to your law." Therefore the Jews said to him, "It is not lawful for us to put anyone to death," 32that the word of Jesus might be fulfilled, which he spoke, signifying by what kind of death he should die.

33Pilate therefore entered again into the Praetorium, called Jesus, and said to him, "Are you the King of the Jews?" 34Jesus answered him, "Do you say this by yourself, or did others tell you about me?" 35Pilate answered, "I'm not a Jew, am I? Your own nation and the chief priests delivered you to me. What have you done?" 36Jesus answered, "My Kingdom is not of this world. If my Kingdom were of this world, then my servants would fight, that I wouldn't be delivered to the Jews. But now my Kingdom is not from here." 37Pilate therefore said to him, "Are you a king then?" Jesus answered, "You say that I am a king. For this reason I have been born, and for this reason I have come into the world, that I should testify to the truth. Everyone who is of the truth listens to my voice." 38Pilate said to him, "What is truth?" When he had said this, he went out again to the Jews, and said to them, "I find no basis for a charge against him. 39But you have a custom, that I should release someone to you at the Passover. Therefore do you want me to release to you the King of the Jews?" 40Then they all shouted again, saying, "Not this man, but Barabbas!" Now Barabbas was a robber.

* * * * * * * * * * * * *

JIM'S THOUGHT FOR THE DAY

Pilate ask, "What is truth?" vs. 38

Pilate's question was probably asked in jest. He was a cynic.

Jesus states that He is truth. His reason for coming into the world: "For this reason I have been born, and for this reason I have come into the world, that I should testify to the truth."

Pilate was being blackmailed by the Jewish religious leaders. They would report him to Caesar if he did not do with Jesus as they insisted. Pilate could find no fault in Jesus yet he gave the command to crucify him. His attempt to comprise by using Barabbas was a sign of his weakness.

Pilate could not handle truth.

Jesus is "The Truth". And the truth sets us free!

Are you willing to follow the truth?

CHALLENGE: TO HAVE TRUTH LIGHT MY WAY AND MAKE ME FREE INDEED.

Prayer:

LORD, I thank you for being truth, for giving truth and for sharing truth. Help me to receive your truth with praise. Amen.

DAILY DEVOTIONAL 62

Scriptures Reading: John 19:1-15

JESUS: THE PASSOVER LAMB

1So Pilate then took Jesus, and flogged him. 2The soldiers twisted thorns into a crown, and put it on his head, and dressed him in a purple garment. 3They kept saying, "Hail, King of the Jews!" and they kept slapping him. 4Then Pilate went out again, and said to them, "Behold, I bring him out to you, that you may know that I find no basis for a charge against him."

5Jesus therefore came out, wearing the crown of thorns and the purple garment. Pilate said to them, "Behold, the man!" 6When therefore the chief priests and the officers saw him, they shouted, saying, "Crucify! Crucify!" Pilate said to them, "Take him yourselves, and crucify him, for I find no basis for a charge against him. ...
...8When therefore Pilate heard this saying, he was more afraid. 9He entered into the Praetorium again, and said to Jesus, "Where are you from?" But Jesus gave him no answer. 10Pilate therefore said to him, "Aren't you speaking to me? Don't you know that I have power to release you, and have power to crucify you?" 11Jesus answered, "You would have no power at all against me, unless it were given to you from above. Therefore he who delivered me to you has greater sin." 12At this, Pilate was seeking to release him, but the Jews cried out, saying, "If you release this man, you aren't Caesar's friend! Everyone who makes himself a king speaks against Caesar!"...

... 14Now it was the Preparation Day of the Passover, at about the sixth hour. He said to the Jews, "Behold, your King!" 15They cried out, "Away with him! Away with him! Crucify him!" Pilate said to them, "Shall I crucify your King?" The chief priests answered, "We have no king but Caesar".

* * * * * * * * * *

JIM'S THOUGHT FOR THE DAY

This passage completes the story of Jesus and Pilate. It shows the motivation of Pilate to placate the religious leaders and avoid any negative relationship with Caesar.

But I want to focus on the statement: of John: "Now it was the Preparation Day of the Passover ..." vs. 14

John thought it important to show that Jesus was crucified on the Day of Passover. Jesus is presented as the Passover lamb who was sacrificed for our sins. In John 1 John the Baptist proclaims: "Behold, the Lamb of God, who takes away the sin of the world!" vs. 14. Throughout the Gospel John makes this emphasis.

"For the Son of Man also came not to be served, but to serve, and to give his life as a ransom for many." Mark 10:45

Even freedom has a price, and Jesus paid that price for the believer. The sacrifice of Jesus frees us from the bondage of sin so we can live a life pleasing to God.

"I have been crucified with Christ, and it is no longer I who live, but Christ lives in me. That life which I now live in the flesh, I live by faith in the Son of God, who loved me, and gave himself up for me." Galatians 2:20

Indeed, God has provided the sacrifice! Behold the Lamb!

CHALLENGE: TO UNDERSTAND THE GIFT OF GOD THROUGH HIS SON AS HE LAYS DOWN HIS LIFE FOR ME.

Prayer:

LORD, I want to live for Him who died for me. I will keep my focus on you. Amen.

DAILY DEVOTIONAL 63

Scriptures Reading: John 19:16-30

IT IS FINISHED!

19:16 So then he delivered him to them to be crucified. So they took Jesus and led him away. 17He went out, bearing his cross, to the place called "The Place of a Skull", which is called in Hebrew, "Golgotha", 18where they crucified him, and with him two others, on either side one, and Jesus in the middle.
19Pilate wrote a title also, and put it on the cross. There was written, "JESUS OF NAZARETH, THE KING OF THE JEWS." 20Therefore many of the Jews read this title, for the place where Jesus was crucified was near the city; and it was written in Hebrew, in Latin, and in Greek. 21The chief priests of the Jews therefore said to Pilate, "Don't write, 'The King of the Jews,' but, 'he said, "I am King of the Jews."'"
22Pilate answered, "What I have written, I have written."...

... 25But standing by Jesus' cross were his mother, his mother's sister, Mary the wife of Clopas, and Mary Magdalene. 26Therefore when Jesus saw his mother, and the disciple whom he loved standing there, he said to his mother, "Woman, behold, your son!" 27Then he said to the disciple, "Behold, your mother!" From that hour, the disciple took her to his own home.

28After this, Jesus, seeing that all things were now finished, that the Scripture might be fulfilled, said, "I am thirsty!" 29Now a vessel full of vinegar was set there; so they put a sponge full of the vinegar on hyssop, and held it at his mouth.

30When Jesus therefore had received the vinegar, he said, "It is finished!" Then he bowed his head and gave up his spirit.

* * * * * * * * * * * *

JIM'S THOUGHT FOR THE DAY

The four gospels record seven things that Jesus said from the cross. John records three of them: 3, 5 and 6.
1. Father, forgive them; for they know not what they do.
2. To day shalt thou be with me in paradise.
3. Woman, behold, thy son! Behold, thy mother!
4. My God, my God, why hast thou forsaken me?
5. I thirst.
6. It is finished.
7. Father, into thy hands I commend my spirit.

Most significant is the shout, "It is finished!" Mark says: "Jesus cried out with a loud voice, and gave up the spirit." Mark 15:37. Mark does not record the words of the shout but John does.

The word Jesus shouted literally means "paid in full." It was the word that would be written on a bill when it was paid.

"Jesus paid it all. All to Him I owe."

There is something deeply personal in that shout. Jesus paid my debt. I am justified ("Just as if I'd" never sinned.).

"Sin has left a crimson stain. He washed it white as snow."

The debt of sin has been paid. Jesus has finished the work of redemption. The divine Lamb has taken away the sin of the world.

Hallelujah, What a Savior!

CHALLENGE: TO REJOICE IN GOD'S POWER AND LOVE TO REDEEM ME FROM MY SIN.

Prayer:

LORD, I thank you for your power and love expressed on the cross. Amen.

DAILY DEVOTIONAL 64

Scripture Reading: John 19:31-37

JOHN: A WITNESS TO THE TRUTH

31Therefore the Jews, because it was the Preparation Day, so that the bodies wouldn't remain on the cross on the Sabbath (for that Sabbath was a special one), asked of Pilate that their legs might be broken and that they might be taken away.

32Therefore the soldiers came and broke the legs of the first and of the other who was crucified with him; 33but when they came to Jesus and saw that he was already dead, they didn't break his legs.

34However, one of the soldiers pierced his side with a spear, and immediately blood and water came out. 35He who has seen has testified, and his testimony is true. He knows that he tells the truth, that you may believe.

36For these things happened that the Scripture might be fulfilled, "A bone of him will not be broken."

37Again another Scripture says, "They will look on him whom they pierced."

* * * * * * * * * * * *

JIM'S THOUGHT FOR THE DAY

John concludes the account of the crucifixion with a person testimony of its accuracy and truth. "He who has seen has testified ..." vs. 35. This is John's way of stating that he was there at the crucifixion and personally witnessed these things.

John began this gospel by declaring that the writer had witnessed these events first-hand (John 1:14). This is a claim John will repeat in his letters.

In 1 John: "That which was from the beginning, that which we have heard, that which we have seen with our eyes, that which we saw, and our hands touched, concerning the Word of life (and the life was revealed, and we have seen, and testify, and declare to you the life, the eternal life, which was with the Father, and was revealed to us." 1 John 1:1-2.

In Revelation: "This is the Revelation of Jesus Christ, which God gave him to show to his servants the things which must happen soon, which he sent and made known by his angel to his servant, John, who testified to God's word and of the testimony of Jesus Christ, about everything that he saw." Revelation 1:1,2

"He knows that he tells the truth that you may believe." vs. 35

John states that he was an eye witness to Jesus death. This is not a second hand account. Literally John was there when they crucified his Lord. Later John will remind us that that is the whole reason for telling the story: That you might believe.

CHALLENGE: TO CLAIM THE EVENT OF THE CROSS IN A PERSONAL WAY WITH JOY AND ASSURANCE.

Prayer:

LORD, I stand amazed in the presence of Jesus. Amen.

DAILY DEVOTIONAL 65

Scripture Reading: John 20:38-42

TWO BELIEVERS PROVIDE FOR THE BURIAL OF JESUS

20:38 After these things, Joseph of Arimathaea, being a disciple of Jesus, but secretly for fear of the Jews, asked of Pilate that he might take away Jesus' body.

Pilate gave him permission. He came therefore and took away his body.

39Nicodemus, who at first came to Jesus by night, also came bringing a mixture of myrrh and aloes, about a hundred Roman pounds.

40So they took Jesus' body, and bound it in linen cloths with the spices, as the custom of the Jews is to bury.

41Now in the place where he was crucified there was a garden. In the garden was a new tomb in which no man had ever yet been laid.

42Then, because of the Jews' Preparation Day (for the tomb was near at hand), they laid Jesus there.

* * * * * * * * * * * *

JIM'S THOUGHT FOR THE DAY

Two men step forward to bury the body of Jesus.

One of them we have met before. In John 3 the visit of Nicodemus to Jesus is recorded. Nicodemus came one night as a seeker for truth. Jesus told him that to enter the Kingdom of God he "must be born again." The climatic verse is John 3:16: "For God so loved the world that he gave his one and only Son, that whoever believes in him should not perish, but have eternal life."

The response of Nicodemus that night is not told. Later when Jesus is being criticized and condemned, Nicodemus speaks up for him wondering why Jesus is being condemned without a hearing. (John 7:50-51).

There is no mention of Nicodemus trusting in Jesus or becoming a follower. But here, following the crucifixion, Nicodemus comes forward as a believer and brings spices for the burial of Jesus.
Joseph of Arimathaea is unknown in scripture until this mention. He is identified as a "disciple of Jesus", but "secretively". Joseph provides a tomb for the burial of Jesus.

I cannot help but wonder about what occurred in the lives of these two men in the times that followed. They are not mentioned again in the scriptures or in church history as far as I know. But for such a time as this they came forward.

This is another instance of the provision of our Heavenly Father. He is always sufficient!

CHALLENGE: TO ALWAYS BE READY TO BE USED OF GOD TO MEET THE NEEDS OF OTHERS IN MY LIFE.

Prayer:

LORD, I want to have eyes that see those in need and ears to hear their cries for help. Amen.

DAILY DEVOTIONAL 66

Scripture Reading: John 20:1-17

WHEN JESUS CALLS YOUR NAME

20.1. Now on the first day of the week, Mary Magdalene went early, while it was still dark, to the tomb, and saw that the stone had been taken away from the tomb. 2Therefore she ran and came to Simon Peter and to the other disciple whom Jesus loved, and said to them, "They have taken away the Lord out of the tomb, and we don't know where they have laid him!" ...

...11But Mary was standing outside at the tomb weeping. So as she wept, she stooped and looked into the tomb, 12and she saw two angels in white sitting, one at the head and one at the feet, where the body of Jesus had lain. 13They asked her, "Woman, why are you weeping?"
She said to them, "Because they have taken away my Lord, and I don't know where they have laid him." 14When she had said this, she turned around and saw Jesus standing, and didn't know that it was Jesus.

15Jesus said to her, "Woman, why are you weeping? Who are you looking for?"
She, supposing him to be the gardener, said to him, "Sir, if you have carried him away, tell me where you have laid him, and I will take him away."

16Jesus said to her, "Mary."

She turned and said to him, "Rabboni!" which is to say, "Teacher!"
17Jesus said to her, "Don't hold me, for I haven't yet ascended to my Father; but go to my brothers and tell them, 'I am ascending to my Father and your Father, to my God and your God.'"

* * * * * * * * * * * *

JIM'S THOUGHT FOR THE DAY

"Jesus said to her, 'Mary.'" vs. 16

Mary Magdalene is an interesting person. There has been much speculation as to whether she was the Mary who anointed Jesus' feet with perfume. Was she the sister of Martha and Lazarus? Was she once a prostitute? She is identified as the Mary who had seven demons cast out of her. We can ask more questions than we can find answers. What we can be sure of is that she was now a devout follower of Jesus. She was present at the crucifixion. She was the first person to see the risen Christ.

The story told in our scripture reading today pivots when Jesus calls her name. The risen Christ had spoken to her outside the garden ton but she did not recognize Him. Probably in her grief she was hiding her face in hands weeping. But everything changed when Jesus called her name.

"Mary!"

In John 1 we read that Jesus knew Nathaniel before they had ever met. Nathaniel is amazed that Jesus knew him. "Nathanael said to him, "How do you know me?" John 1:41.

Jesus knows me! Jesus knows you! And he not only knows you, he loves you!

I have no doubt that when you and I meet Jesus one day, He will call us by our names

CHALLENGE: TO REJOICE IN KNOWING THAT JESUS KNOWS ALL ABOUT ME AND LOVES ME ANYWAY.

Prayer:

LORD, I pray in your name as you taught me to do. Thank you for knowing my name. Amen.

DAILY DEVOTIONAL 67

Scripture Reading: John 20:18-42

MY LORD AND MY GOD!

20:18 Mary Magdalene came and told the disciples that she had seen the Lord, and that he had said these things to her. 19When therefore it was evening on that day, the first day of the week, and when the doors were locked where the disciples were assembled, for fear of the Jews, Jesus came and stood in the middle and said to them, "Peace be to you."
20When he had said this, he showed them his hands and his side. The disciples therefore were glad when they saw the Lord. 21Jesus therefore said to them again, "Peace be to you. As the Father has sent me, even so I send you." ...
... 24But Thomas, one of the twelve, called Didymus, wasn't with them when Jesus came. 25The other disciples therefore said to him, "We have seen the Lord!"But he said to them, "Unless I see in his hands the print of the nails, put my finger into the print of the nails, and put my hand into his side, I will not believe."
26After eight days, again his disciples were inside and Thomas was with them. Jesus came, the doors being locked, and stood in the middle, and said, "Peace be to you." 27Then he said to Thomas, "Reach here your finger, and see my hands. Reach here your hand, and put it into my side. Don't be unbelieving, but believing."

28Thomas answered him, "My Lord and my God!"

29Jesus said to him, "Because you have seen me, you have believed. Blessed are those who have not seen and have believed." 30Therefore Jesus did many other signs in the presence of his disciples, which are not written in this book; 31but these are written that you may believe that Jesus is the Christ, the Son of God, and that believing you may have life in his name.

* * * * * * * * * * * * * *

JIM'S THOUGHT FOR THE DAY

Thomas. What is the first word that comes to your mind when you hear his name?

Probably "Doubting Thomas". He has been stuck with that word ever since Resurrection night.

I wonder why Thomas was not with the disciples that night. The scriptures do not tell us why. They simply say Thomas "wasn't with them when Jesus came." vs. 24 It is fruitless for us to speculate about this but somehow I think it was related to his unbelieving heart.

When told by the disciples that they had seen the Lord, Thomas replied, "Unless I see in his hands the print of the nails, put my finger into the print of the nails, and put my hand into his side, I will not believe." vs. 25

A week later Jesus appears again to the disciples with Thomas present. Jesus said directly to Thomas, "Reach here your finger, and see my hands. Reach here your hand, and put it into my side. Don't be unbelieving, but believing."

The scripture does not say that Thomas touched the hands or the side of Jesus. Instead it says Thomas said, "My Lord and my God". From doubting to believing! Thomas does not deserve a bad rap. From now on I am going to call him "Believing Thomas!"

CHALLENGE: TO BE A BELIEVING FOLLOWER OF JESUS BECAUSE HE IS MY LORD AND MY GOD.

Prayer:

LORD, I pray for your patience with me when my faith is weak.
Amen.

DAILY DEVOTIONAL 68

Scripture Reading: John 21:1-14

JESUS REVEALED HIMSELF TO THE DISCIPLES

21.1After these things, Jesus revealed himself again to the disciples at the sea of Tiberias. He revealed himself this way. 2Simon Peter, Thomas called Didymus, Nathanael of Cana in Galilee, and the sons of Zebedee, and two others of his disciples were together. 3Simon Peter said to them, "I'm going fishing."

They told him, "We are also coming with you." They immediately went out and entered into the boat. That night, they caught nothing. 4But when day had already come, Jesus stood on the beach; yet the disciples didn't know that it was Jesus. 5Jesus therefore said to them, "Children, have you anything to eat?"

They answered him, "No."

6He said to them, "Cast the net on the right side of the boat, and you will find some."

They cast it therefore, and now they weren't able to draw it in for the multitude of fish. 7That disciple therefore whom Jesus loved said to Peter, "It's the Lord!"

So when Simon Peter heard that it was the Lord, he wrapped his coat around himself (for he was naked), and threw himself into the sea. 8But the other disciples came in the little boat (for they were not far from the land, but about two hundred cubits away), dragging the net full of fish. 9So when they got out on the land, they saw a fire of coals there, with fish and bread laid on it. 10Jesus said to them, "Bring some of the fish which you have just caught."

11Simon Peter went up, and drew the net to land, full of one hundred fifty-three great fish. Even though there were so many, the net wasn't torn.

12Jesus said to them, "Come and eat breakfast!"

None of the disciples dared inquire of him, "Who are you?" knowing that it was the Lord. ...

* * * * * * * * * * * *

JIM'S THOUGHT FOR THE DAY

What were the disciples to do now? Everything changed with the resurrection of Jesus.

Peter decided to go fishing and some of the disciples went with him.

At a time when the disciples needed direction and assurance, Jesus shows up.

Jesus shows concern about their lack of fishing luck. He gives them some directions and they catch a large number of fish.

Then Jesus provided their breakfast.

Jesus is the great provider.

Whether the needs of his followers are physical or spiritual, He provides.

Paul experienced this: "My God will supply (provide) every need of yours according to his riches in glory in Christ Jesus." Philippians 4:19

CHALLENGE: TO FIND THE CERTAINTY OF HIS PROVISION IN EVERY AREA OF LIFE.

Prayer:

LORD, Thank you for supplying my every need. Amen.

DAILY DEVOTIONAL 69

Scripture Reading: John 21:15-19

JESUS' QUESTION: DO YOU LOVE ME?

21:15So when they had eaten their breakfast, Jesus said to Simon Peter, "Simon, son of Jonah, do you love me more than these?"

He said to him, "Yes, Lord; you know that I have affection for you." He said to him, "Feed my lambs."

16He said to him again a second time, "Simon, son of Jonah, do you love me?"

He said to him, "Yes, Lord; you know that I have affection for you." He said to him, "Tend my sheep."

17He said to him the third time, "Simon, son of Jonah, do you have affection for me?"

Peter was grieved because he asked him the third time, "Do you have affection for me?" He said to him, "Lord, you know everything. You know that I have affection for you."

Jesus said to him, "Feed my sheep. 18Most certainly I tell you, when you were young, you dressed yourself and walked where you wanted to. But when you are old, you will stretch out your hands, and another will dress you and carry you where you don't want to go."

19Now he said this, signifying by what kind of death he would glorify God.

When he had said this, he said to him, "Follow me."

* * * * * * * * * * *

JIM'S THOUGHT FOR THE DAY

"Simon, son of Jonah, do you love me?" vs. 16

You are familiar with this passage. Two different words for love are used in this exchange between Jesus and Peter.

The first two times Jesus ask the question to Peter, "Do you love me?" Jesus uses the word for love (agapa) that means total and unreserved devotion. Peter answers the question using the word for love (phileo) that means affection or friendship.

The World English Bible translates the passage this way:
Jesus: "Do you love me?"
Peter: "You know that I have affection for you."

Why did Peter not use the love word meaning total and unreserved devotion? I think it was because of his embarrassment over having denied Jesus three times on the night before the crucifixion. He did not feel worth to say he loved Jesus with total and unreserved devotion. He must have still been lamenting his denials of knowing Jesus after having boasted that he would never deny Him.

The third time Jesus ask Peter the question, Jesus used the love word for affection or friendship.

But Jesus indicates His forgiveness and grace with this invitation to Peter, "Follow me." Jesus wanted Peter to know of his forgiveness and love.

CHALLENGE: TO GROW IN MY LOVE FOR JESUS UNTIL IT IS TRULY TOTAL AND UNRESERVED.

Prayer:

LORD, I want to express my love for you in both words and deeds.

DAILY DEVOTIONAL 70

Scripture Reading: John 21:20-25

THE DISCIPLE WHOM JESUS LOVED

21/:20 Then Peter, turning around, saw a disciple following. This was the disciple whom Jesus loved, the one who had also leaned on Jesus' breast at the supper and asked, "Lord, who is going to betray you?"

21Peter, seeing him, said to Jesus, "Lord, what about this man?"

22Jesus said to him, "If I desire that he stay until I come, what is that to you? You follow me."

23This saying therefore went out among the brothers that this disciple wouldn't die. Yet Jesus didn't say to him that he wouldn't die, but, "If I desire that he stay until I come, what is that to you?"

24This is the disciple who testifies about these things, and wrote these things. We know that his witness is true.

25There are also many other things which Jesus did, which if they would all be written, I suppose that even the world itself wouldn't have room for the books that would be written.

* * * * * * * * * * * * * *

JIM'S THOUGHT FOR THE DAY

"This was the disciple whom Jesus loved." vs. 20

We have previously noted that John in his gospel speaks of himself in the third person. Here he calls himself again "the disciple whom Jesus loved." He uses this phrase six times in the gospel.

John did not mean that He thought Jesus loved him more than he loved others. This was John's way of expressing the deep personal love Jesus had showed to him.

I hope you are experiencing the love of God in Christ Jesus. The Gospel of John is a book about how "God so loved the world that He gave his only Son that whosoever believes in Him might not perish but have eternal life." John 3:16

The gospel song says:
"I am so glad that Jesus loves me!"

"Jesus loves me, This I know.
For the Bible tells me so."

I am one that Jesus loves!

You are one that Jesus loves!

What a way to end the gospel story.

CHALLENGE: TO REFLECT ON THE LOVE OF JESUS FOR ME AND TO COMMIT MY LIFE TO FOLLOWING AND LOVING HIM.

Prayer:

LORD, I love you. Amen.

Made in the USA
Middletown, DE
03 August 2022

70309045R00086